Active Reading Strategies

Teruhiko Kadoyama

LiveABC editors

Book 1

JN061737

CEFR
A2

 SEIBIDO LiveABC

photographs

iStockphoto

音声ファイルのダウンロード／ストリーミング

CD マーク表示がある箇所は、音声を弊社 HP より無料でダウンロード／ストリーミングすることができます。下記 URL の書籍詳細ページに音声ダウンロードアイコンがございますのでそちらから自習用音声としてご活用ください。

https://www.seibido.co.jp/ad690

Active Reading Strategies Book 1

CONTENTS

Active Reading Strategies Book 1

CONTENT CHART

VOCABULARY BUILDER	LANGUAGE NOTES	PUT IT IN WRITING
Words With Different Meanings	Quantifiers	• Write about an unforgettable trip • Plan a two-day trip
Suffixes: *-er/-or*	Modal Verbs	• Write about a show that you have been to • Create your own piece of music
Collocations of *Come*	Sense Verbs	• Write a brief sequel to *The Bremen Town Musicians* • Write a novel/movie review
Prefixes: *il-/im-/in-/ir-*	Coordinate Conjunctions	• Write about the laws or rules in your country • Create a list of interesting facts about a country of your choice
Suffix: *-al*	Conjunctive Adverbs	• Write about a baseball player's day • Create a timeline of important events for a sport or a sports player
Measure Words	Imperatives	• Write a recipe • Create a food diary entry
Words With Different Meanings	Infinitives	• Answer questions about a flyer • Describe a painting
Suffix: *-ness*	Gerunds	• Complete a mind map about gadgets • Write a paragraph based on your gadget mind map
Adult and Baby Animals	Comparative and Superlative Adjectives	• Write about three endangered animals' habitats and the reasons they are threatened • Create a poster to help protect a threatened animal
Collocations of *Get*	*That*-Clauses	• Write about belief words with the suffix *-ism* • Try minimalism for yourself and share your experience
Collocations of *Out*	Conjunction—*When*	• Write your own joke • Make inferences based on a song or a poem
Words With Different Meanings	Passive Voice	• Write about a kind of technology that has changed the world • Invent a new product

LEARNING OVERVIEW

Active Reading Strategies Book 1 is the first volume of the *Active Reading Strategies* series. Each book is divided into 12 striking units with a review section after every six units. Each unit contains a warm-up section, reading passage, reading comprehension questions, two vocabulary building exercises, language notes, and reading skill information with relevant exercises. A writing exercise paired with a relevant real-life activity wraps up each unit and provides students with an opportunity for further practice and learning. With our systematic learning methods and a variety of practical content, students will gain competence throughout the series.

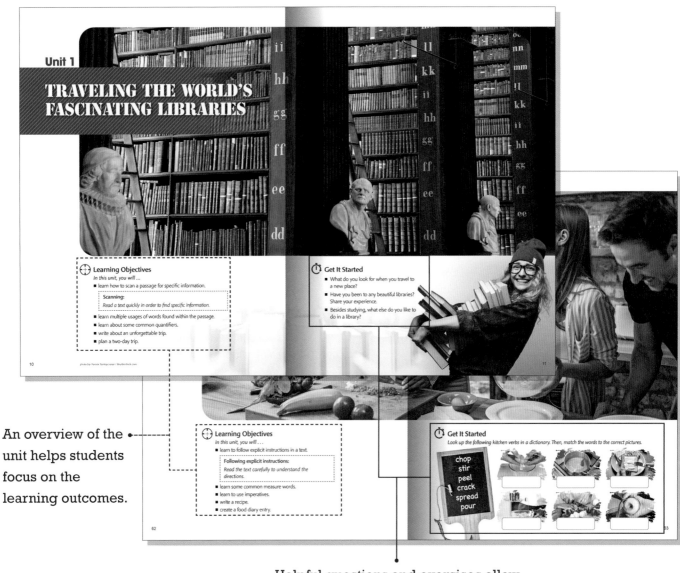

An overview of the unit helps students focus on the learning outcomes.

Helpful questions and exercises allow teachers to front-load the unit topic.

READING

This section contains a selected reading passage followed by interesting facts and critical thinking questions. After that, the reading comprehension, vocabulary, and grammar sections are presented to enhance students' reading fluency.

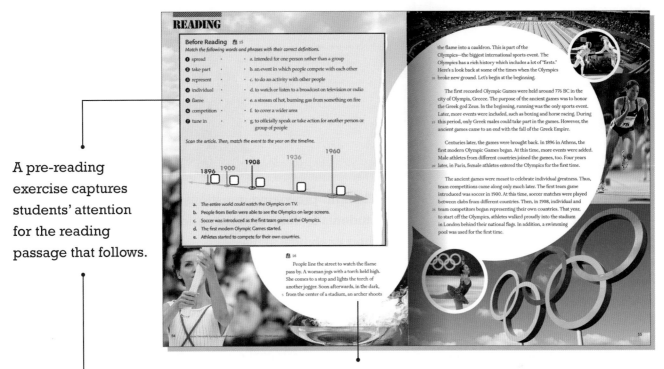

A pre-reading exercise captures students' attention for the reading passage that follows.

The diverse text structures and themes increase students' interest.

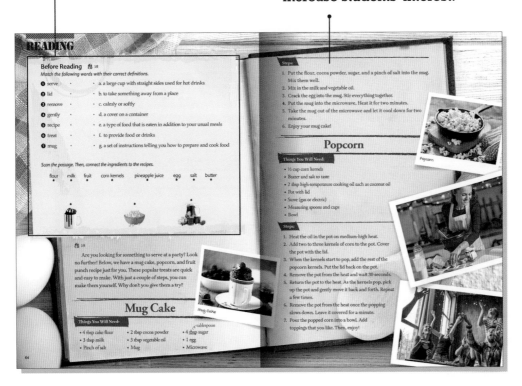

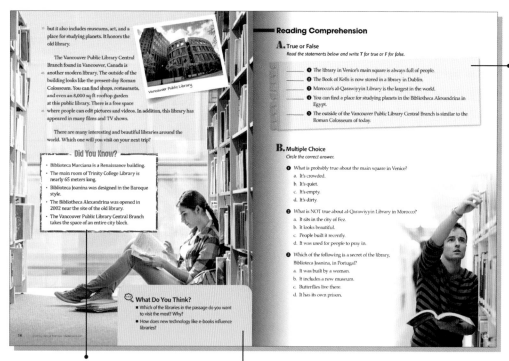

• A variety of reading comprehension questions tests and boosts students' understanding of the passage.

Additional fun facts and useful information help students gain knowledge in a fun way.

• Thought-provoking questions allow students to think critically and improve their analytical skills.

A basic exercise is provided to assess students' understanding of the unit's vocabulary and phrases.

Applicable grammar usage along with practice exercises helps students comprehend the structures of the text.

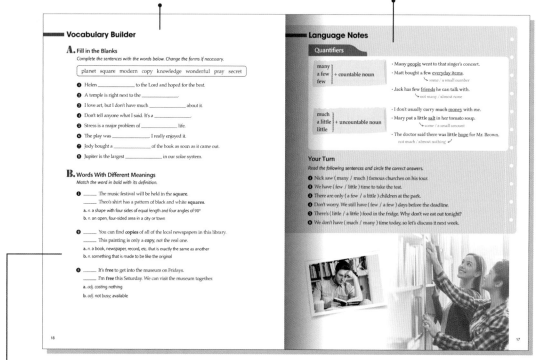

An advanced exercise is presented to broaden students' vocabulary.

READING SKILL

This section contains a brief explanation of the targeted reading skill with relevant exercises. Students can apply the reading strategy to read effectively.

PUT IT IN WRITING

Two writing exercises are provided to take students to a higher language proficiency. Students can put their thoughts into words and practice a mix of language skills.

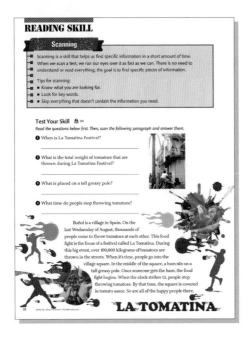

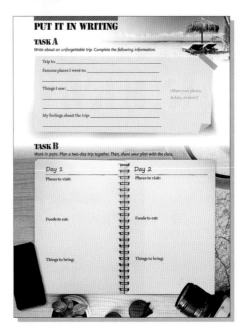

REVIEW

A review section after every six units is offered to check students' vocabulary, grammar, and reading competencies. This section incorporates a variety of reading comprehension questions along with reading skills. It provides an excellent tool for students to track their improvements and understand their reading comprehension levels.

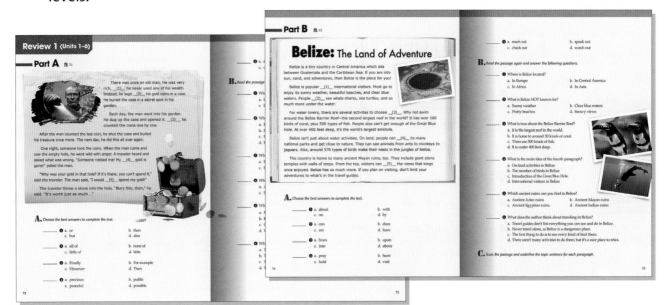

Unit 1

TRAVELING THE WORLD'S FASCINATING LIBRARIES

⊕ Learning Objectives

In this unit, you will ...

- learn how to scan a passage for specific information.

> **Scanning:**
>
> *Read a text quickly in order to find specific information.*

- learn multiple usages of words found within the passage.
- learn about some common quantifiers.
- write about an unforgettable trip.
- plan a two-day trip.

⏱ Get It Started

- What do you look for when you travel to a new place?

- Have you been to any beautiful libraries? Share your experience.

- Besides studying, what else do you like to do in a library?

READING

Before Reading 🎧 02

Match the following words and phrases with their correct definitions.

❶ fascinating · · a. happening or existing now

❷ pray · · b. to start an organization, especially by giving money

❸ jail · · c. to show great respect for someone or something

❹ found · · d. very interesting

❺ honor · · e. a prison

❻ present · · f. besides

❼ in addition · · g. to speak to God in order to ask for help

Biblioteca marciana

Scan the second and fifth paragraphs. Then, answer the following questions.

❶ **(paragraph 2)** What can you see on the walls and ceilings of Biblioteca Marciana?

_____

❷ **(paragraph 2)** How many books does the library of Dublin have?

_____

❸ **(paragraph 5)** What can you see on the roof of the Vancouver Public Library Central Branch?

_____

Trinity College Library

🎧 03

On trips, people usually want to shop or see famous places. They don't normally think about reading or studying. However, there are many fascinating and beautiful libraries around the world.
5 If you visit one, you might want to include more in your travels.

Here are some historical libraries you can visit. In Venice's main square, people are everywhere, so there are few quiet places. However, its library, Biblioteca
10 Marciana, doesn't have many people in it. This library

has wonderful paintings on its walls and ceilings, too. In Dublin, there is a large library called Trinity College Library. Its main room holds over 200,000 books. It also
15 has the Book of Kells—a beautiful copy of the Bible. If you want to see a very old and beautiful library, go to Morocco. Al-Qarawiyyin Library is the oldest in the world located in the city of Fez. Fatima al-Fihri founded it for the public to study and pray in.

Al-Qarawiyyin Library

20 Another historical library is in Portugal. Many artists worked together to make the University Library in Coimbra, Biblioteca Joanina, beautiful. This library has a few secrets. First, it has its own jail called the Academic Prison! Students once
25 stayed there if they broke the rules. The second secret is—bats live inside the library. The bats are meant to eat the insects that eat books.

Biblioteca Joanina

You can also see more modern libraries. There was once a very famous library in Alexandria,
30 Egypt, which was named the Great Library of Alexandria. However, it declined over a number of centuries, and all the knowledge in it was lost. Now, there is a new, modern library called the Bibliotheca Alexandrina. It contains many books,

Bibliotheca Alexandrina

35 but it also includes museums, art, and a
place for studying planets. It honors the
old library.

The Vancouver Public Library Central
Branch found in Vancouver, Canada is
40 another modern library. The outside of the
building looks like the present-day Roman
Colosseum. You can find shops, restaurants,
and even an 8,000 sq-ft rooftop garden
at this public library. There is a free space
45 where people can edit pictures and videos. In addition, this library has
appeared in many films and TV shows.

There are many interesting and beautiful libraries around the
world. Which one will you visit on your next trip?

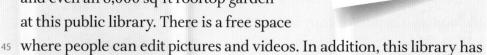
Vancouver Public Library

Did You Know?

- Biblioteca Marciana is a Renaissance building.
- The main room of Trinity College Library is nearly 65 meters long.
- Biblioteca Joanina was designed in the Baroque style.
- The Bibliotheca Alexandrina was opened in 2002 near the site of the old library.
- The Vancouver Public Library Central Branch takes the space of an entire city block.

What Do You Think?

- Which of the libraries in the passage do you want to visit the most? Why?
- How does new technology like e-books influence libraries?

Reading Comprehension

A. True or False

*Read the statements below and write **T** for true or **F** for false.*

_____ ❶ The library in Venice's main square is always full of people.

_____ ❷ The Book of Kells is now stored in a library in Dublin.

_____ ❸ Morocco's al-Qarawiyyin Library is the largest in the world.

_____ ❹ You can find a place for studying planets in the Bibliotheca Alexandrina in Egypt.

_____ ❺ The outside of the Vancouver Public Library Central Branch is similar to the Roman Colosseum of today.

B. Multiple Choice

Circle the correct answer.

❶ What is probably true about the main square in Venice?
   a. It's crowded.
   b. It's quiet.
   c. It's empty.
   d. It's dirty.

❷ What is NOT true about al-Qarawiyyin Library in Morocco?
   a. It sits in the city of Fez.
   b. It looks beautiful.
   c. People built it recently.
   d. It was used for people to pray in.

❸ Which of the following is a secret of the library, Biblioteca Joanina, in Portugal?
   a. It was built by a woman.
   b. It includes a new museum.
   c. Butterflies live there.
   d. It has its own prison.

Vocabulary Builder

A. Fill in the Blanks

Complete the sentences with the words below. Change the forms if necessary.

> planet   square   modern   copy   knowledge   wonderful   pray   secret

❶ Helen _____ to the Lord and hoped for the best.

❷ A temple is right next to the _____.

❸ I love art, but I don't have much _____ about it.

❹ Don't tell anyone what I said. It's a _____.

❺ Stress is a major problem of _____ life.

❻ The play was _____. I really enjoyed it.

❼ Jody bought a _____ of the book as soon as it came out.

❽ Jupiter is the largest _____ in our solar system.

B. Words With Different Meanings

Match the word in bold with its definition.

❶ _____ The music festival will be held in the **square**.

  _____ Theo's shirt has a pattern of black and white **squares**.

  a. *n.* a shape with four sides of equal length and four angles of 90°

  b. *n.* an open, four-sided area in a city or town

❷ _____ You can find **copies** of all of the local newspapers in this library.

  _____ This painting is only a **copy**, not the real one.

  a. *n.* a book, newspaper, record, etc. that is exactly the same as another

  b. *n.* something that is made to be like the original

❸ _____ It's **free** to get into the museum on Fridays.

  _____ I'm **free** this Saturday. We can visit the museum together.

  a. *adj.* costing nothing

  b. *adj.* not busy; available

Language Notes

Quantifiers

many a few few } + countable noun

- **Many** <u>people</u> went to that singer's concert.
- Matt bought **a few** <u>everyday items</u>.
  ↘ some / a small number
- Jack has **few** <u>friends</u> he can talk with.
  ↘ not many / almost none

much a little little } + uncountable noun

- I don't usually carry **much** <u>money</u> with me.
- Mary put **a little** <u>salt</u> in her tomato soup.
  ↘ some / a small amount
- The doctor said there was **little** <u>hope</u> for Mr. Brown.
  not much / almost nothing ↙

Your Turn

Read the following sentences and circle the correct answers.

❶ Nick saw (many / much) famous churches on his tour.

❷ We have (few / little) time to take the test.

❸ There are only (a few / a little) children at the park.

❹ Don't worry. We still have (few / a few) days before the deadline.

❺ There's (little / a little) food in the fridge. Why don't we eat out tonight?

❻ We don't have (much / many) time today, so let's discuss it next week.

READING SKILL

Scanning is a skill that helps us find specific information in a short amount of time. When we scan a text, we run our eyes over it as fast as we can. There is no need to understand or read everything; the goal is to find specific pieces of information.

Tips for scanning:
- Know what you are looking for.
- Look for key words.
- Skip everything that doesn't contain the information you need.

Test Your Skill 🎧 04

Read the questions below first. Then, scan the following paragraph and answer them.

❶ When is La Tomatina Festival?

_____

❷ What is the total weight of tomatoes that are thrown during La Tomatina Festival?

_____

❸ What is placed on a tall greasy pole?

_____

❹ What time do people stop throwing tomatoes?

_____

Buñol is a village in Spain. On the last Wednesday of August, thousands of people come to throw tomatoes at each other. This food fight is the focus of a festival called La Tomatina. During this big event, over 100,000 kilograms of tomatoes are thrown in the streets. When it's time, people go into the village square. In the middle of the square, a ham sits on a tall greasy pole. Once someone gets the ham, the food fight begins. When the clock strikes 12, people stop throwing tomatoes. By that time, the square is covered in tomato sauce. So are all of the happy people there.

LA TOMATINA

photo by: Iakov Filimonov / Shutterstock.com

PUT IT IN WRITING

TASK A

Write about an unforgettable trip. Complete the following information.

Trip to: _____

Famous places I went to: _____
_____

Things I saw: _____
_____
_____

(Share your photos, tickets, or more!)

My feelings about the trip: _____
_____

TASK B

Work in pairs. Plan a two-day trip together. Then, share your plan with the class.

Day 1

Places to visit:

Foods to eat:

Things to bring:

Day 2

Places to visit:

Foods to eat:

Things to bring:

UNIT 2

STOMP: MUSIC TO SEE AND HEAR

⊕ **Learning Objectives**

In this unit, you will . . .

- learn how to identify topic sentences.

> **Identifying topic sentences:**
>
> *Read a paragraph to find the sentence that holds the main idea.*

- learn the suffixes, *-er/-or.*
- learn about modal verbs.
- write about a show that you have been to.
- create your own piece of music.

⏱ Get It Started

- Look at the picture. What do you think these people are doing?
- Listen to the audio. How do you think these sounds were made? 💿 05
- Do you know any of the following instruments? Do you play any of them?

READING

Before Reading 🎧 06

Match the following words and phrases with their correct definitions.

1. ordinary •   • a. to clean something, especially a floor

2. broom •   • b. to look at someone or something
                         because they are interesting or attractive

3. check out •   • c. a brush with a long handle, used for cleaning
                         the floor

4. barely •   • d. almost not

5. contain •   • e. usual

6. sweep •   • f. in place of someone or something else

7. instead •   • g. to control or hide a strong emotion,
                         such as excitement or anger

Scan the article and underline topic sentence for each paragraph. Then, check (✓) the general idea of the article below.

General idea of the article:
- ☐ When *Stomp* started
- ☐ General introduction of *Stomp*
- ☐ How to play music with everyday items
- ☐ The feelings that a *Stomp* show gives you

🎧 07

When you look at a broom, you probably think of cleaning. When you look at a basketball, you probably think of sports. For most people, these things are very ordinary. However, some people use these everyday
5 items for something different—they use them to make music and create a unique type of art.

Stomp is a music show. The performers play music, but they don't use
10 guitars or pianos. Instead, they use things like pipes, chairs, and bottles.

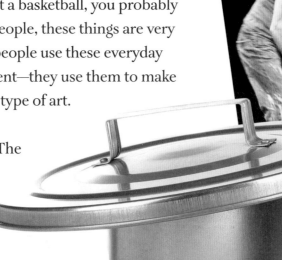

photo by: A.RICARDO, Ferenc Szelepcsenyi / Shutterstock.com

They also use parts of their bodies like their
hands and feet. Sometimes, they even use apples!
15 *Stomp* started in England in 1991 with two people,
Luke Cresswell and Steve McNicholas. Their first
show was at the Edinburgh Festival Fringe in Edinburgh,
Scotland. *Stomp* grew from there.

These days, there are *Stomp* shows all around the world. The
20 show sometimes tours to places like Cape Town, Bremen, and
Guatemala City. You can even check out a *Stomp* show in one of
the Off-Broadway theaters in New York City. Indeed, *Stomp* has
been performed in important shows like the London Olympics
closing ceremony in 2012.

25 Here is an idea of what a *Stomp* performance is like. A man
comes out with a broom and begins to sweep the stage floor.
Then, he starts to tap out a rhythm with his broom. You can
hear the quiet striking as though he's thinking of something else.
Slowly, more people join him on stage while drumming their
30 brooms to the same beat. The banging gets louder and faster.
Soon you can barely contain yourself. You want to jump up and
dance to match your heartbeat to the rhythm of the brooms.

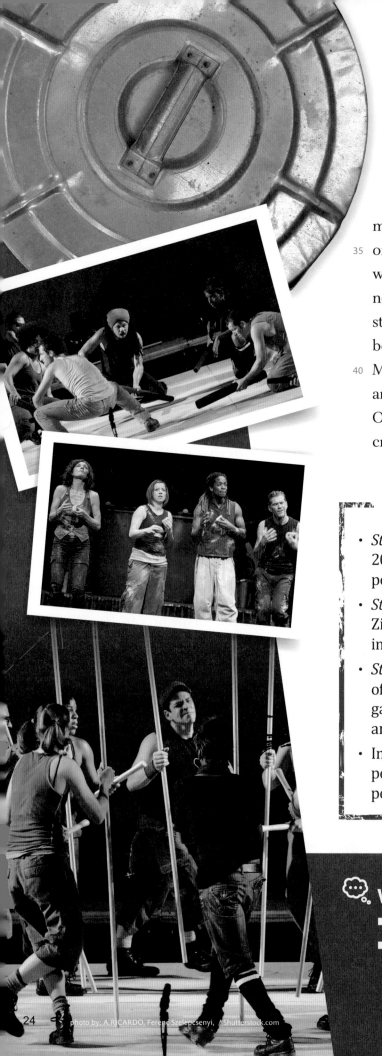

The performers of *Stomp* want you to hear music and see art in new places. They take
35 ordinary things and use them in unordinary ways. Sometimes, if you look at the world in a new way like *Stomp* performers do, you might start to think differently, and your life will become different. Art is not only in museums.
40 Music is not only in concert halls. These things are all around us. We just have to look for them. Open your mind—you might be the next big creator.

Did You Know?

- *Stomp* has been performed over 20,000 times to more than 12 million people.
- *Stomp* sometimes uses matchboxes, Zippo lighters, and hammer handles in their performances.
- *Stomp* has used about 50,000 boxes of matches, 30,000 brooms, 20,000 garbage cans, 10,000 drumsticks, and 25,000 liters of black paint.
- In the largest official *Stomp* performance, there were 40 performers from 12 different countries.

What Do You Think?

- Do you know any unusual musical instruments?
- What are your body's reactions when you hear the beat of drums? How do you feel?

Reading Comprehension

A. True or False

Read the statements below and write T for true or F for false.

_____ ❶ The *Stomp* performers play music with ordinary instruments like guitars and pianos.

_____ ❷ *Stomp* was created in England by Luke Cresswell and Steve McNicholas.

_____ ❸ *Stomp* started in London in 2012.

_____ ❹ *Stomp* performances are usually very quiet.

_____ ❺ The author thinks we just have to look around us for art.

B. Short Answers

Read the following questions and write down your answers.

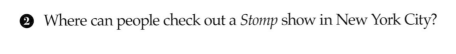

❶ When was *Stomp* created?

_____

❷ Where can people check out a *Stomp* show in New York City?

_____

❸ What is the main idea of the fourth paragraph?

_____

❹ What happens if you start to think differently?

_____

C. Identify Referents

Check what the following words in bold refer to.

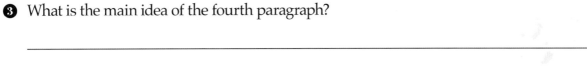

❶ **these things** (paragraph 1, line 3)
- ☐ sports
- ☐ music and art
- ☐ a broom and a basketball

❷ **they** (paragraph 2, line 11)
- ☐ the *Stomp* performers
- ☐ pipes, chairs, and bottles
- ☐ Luke Cresswell and Steve McNicholas

❸ **them** (paragraph 5, line 41)
- ☐ art and music
- ☐ museums
- ☐ concert halls

Vocabulary Builder

A. Fill in the Blanks

Complete the sentences with the words and phrases below. Change the forms if necessary.

> beat create part loud unique tour pipe look for

❶ Sarah doesn't just make a dress; she _____ a work of art.

❷ The explosion was caused by a leaking gas _____.

❸ The TV is too _____. Please turn it down.

❹ Dolly dropped her key, so she started to _____ it on the ground.

❺ The people at the party all danced to the _____ of the music.

❻ The show is going to _____ throughout Europe next year.

❼ The clock is _____; it is unlike any other.

❽ My office is in a central _____ of town.

B. Suffixes: *-er/-or*

*The suffixes **-er/-or** mean "person." Look at the examples in the left column. Then, circle the correct answers in the right column.*

- dancer
- performer
- player
- reporter
- actor
- creator
- instructor
- visitor

❶ He is the (create / creator) of many children's toys.

❷ The band (performed / performer) a free concert for the town festival.

❸ Sean wants to be an (act / actor) when he grows up.

❹ You have some (visit / visitors) to see you.

❺ Tourists are (instructed / instructors) not to travel to the area.

❻ The little girl was (playing / player) with her toys.

❼ I never knew you were such a good (dance / dancer).

❽ Other researchers (reported / reporters) similar results.

Language Notes

Modal Verbs

S. + modal verb (+ not) + V.

- They can play soccer well.
  ↳ to show ability

- It may/might rain tomorrow.
  ↳ to show possibility

- You shouldn't eat too much sugar.
  ↳ to give a strong suggestion

modal verb + S. + V. ?

- May/Can/Could I have another drink?
  ↳ to ask for permission

- Will you close the window, please?
  ↳ to ask someone to do something

- Shall we go to the movie now?
  ↳ to give a suggestion

lesser possibility ←——|——|——→ higher possibility

might   may

Usage	Modal Verbs
ability	can, could
suggestion	can, could, shall
request	can, could, will, would
permission	can, could, may
possibility	can, could, may, might
advice	should

Your Turn

Read the following sentences and circle the correct answers.

1. Belle didn't come to work today. She might (be / is) sick.
2. It's going to rain. You (should / shouldn't) take your umbrella.
3. I'm looking for the airport. (Can / Should) you tell me where it is?
4. I'm so dizzy. I (shall not / can't) even walk straight.
5. (Could I / Could you) borrow your pen?
6. (Shall we / Shall you) have dinner together?

READING SKILL

Identifying Topic Sentences

A topic sentence is a sentence that shows the main idea of the paragraph in a general way. It organizes the paragraph and acts as a core from which the paragraph develops. The topic sentence is often the first sentence of a paragraph. However, sometimes it can also be found in the middle or at the end.

Test Your Skill 🎧 08

Read the following passage and underline the topic sentence of the first three paragraphs.

Music is very good. Most people like to listen to music. Many also like to play music. Listening to music is a lot of fun. You can listen to music when you work. You can listen to it when you are on a bus. You can also listen to it when you are with your friends. Playing music is fun, too. It is fun to play songs with your friends. Music makes people happy. Music is pretty good for your health as well.

Listening to music can make you healthier. For example, if you are stressed, you should listen to music. When you listen to music, your body relaxes. After that, you will feel better. Listening to music can also make you stronger. You should listen to music when you exercise. This will give you more energy. When you have more energy, you will exercise more. You can also listen to music at night. It will help you fall asleep. If you sleep more, you will be healthier.

Music is also very good for your brain. Recently, doctors did a study. They found many people who did not play music. They gave those people a test. Then, those people learned the piano for two weeks. After two weeks, doctors gave the people a second test. The people did much better on the second test.

You should listen to music. You should play music, too. It is good for your body. It is good for your brain. It will also make you happy!

PUT IT IN WRITING

TASK A

Write about a show that you have been to in a 50-word paragraph.
Remember to include a topic sentence.

TASK B

Work in groups. Create your own piece of music using any everyday item or musical instrument and share it with the class. Then, choose your favorite groups and state your reasons below.

Our group name: _____

Name of our music: _____

Things we need: _____

	Favorite Groups	Things the Group Used	Reasons
❶			
❷			
❸			

UNIT 3

THE BREMEN TOWN MUSICIANS

—Adapted from *Grimm's Fairy Tales*

 ## Learning Objectives

In this unit, you will . . .

- learn how to make predictions when reading a text.

  > **Making predictions:**
  >
  > *Guess what is going to happen based on information in the text and your personal experiences.*

- learn the collocations of *come*.
- learn about sense verbs.
- write a brief sequel to *The Bremen Town Musicians*.
- write a movie review.

⏱ Get It Started

- The following are some common characters found in fairy tales. In which stories can you find these characters?

goblin

fairy

witch

elf

giant

talking animal

- What is your favorite story? What is the story about?
- Look at the title *The Bremen Town Musicians* and the pictures. What do you think the story is about?

Before Reading 🎧 09

Match the following words and phrases with their correct definitions.

❶ feed · · a. a way of solving a problem

❷ claw · · b. to leave a place quickly because you are in danger

❸ drown · · c. to make somebody go away by frightening them

❹ flee · · d. somewhere that is far away

❺ distance · · e. a sharp curved nail on an animal

❻ scare away · · f. to give food to a person or animal

❼ solution · · g. to kill somebody by holding them underwater

Read the following text and answer the questions.

❶
> *Once upon a time, there was an old donkey that could no longer work. So, his master thought, "I should stop feeding that donkey." The donkey noticed something was wrong ....*

What do you think the donkey will do next?

_____

❷
> *On the road, the donkey found a crying dog. "What's wrong?" asked the donkey. "I'm too old and can't hunt anymore," the dog explained, "my master wanted to kill me, so I ran away."*

What do you think will happen next?

_____

🎧 10

Once upon a time, there was an old donkey that could no longer work. So, his master thought, "I should stop feeding that donkey." The donkey noticed something

5 was wrong and decided to escape. "I'll go to Bremen and become a musician," said the donkey.

On the road, the donkey found a crying dog. "What's wrong?" asked the donkey. "I'm
10 too old and can't hunt anymore," the dog explained, "my master wanted to kill me, so I ran away." The donkey asked the dog to go to Bremen and be a musician.

Later, they saw an old cat sitting next to
15 the road. She could no longer catch mice because her teeth and claws weren't sharp. The cat's owner wanted to drown her, so she fled. "Where should I go?" asked the cat. The donkey invited her to join them.

20 Eventually, the three friends came across a rooster who was crowing very loudly. It sounded like it was his last song. "Sadly," he told them, "I will be cooked for my owners' supper tomorrow." The rooster was then invited to come along with the group.

25 As the friends were walking, they saw a small house in the distance. They walked towards the house and it became bigger and bigger. They looked inside and saw a warm fire and delicious food on the table. Unfortunately, four thieves were also inside the house. The donkey said, "We should
30 live here! But how do we scare the thieves away?"

They worked together and found a solution. They went to a window. Then, the dog climbed onto the donkey's back, the cat climbed onto the dog's back, and the rooster stood on the cat's head! The four animals
35 started to sing. However, they lost their balance and crashed through the window and into the house. The thieves thought they heard a ghost. Out of fear, they ran away. The animals now had a new home! They went inside, enjoyed the food,
40 and went to sleep.

The thieves were very angry. "We must get our house back," said the leader. He ordered one man to go back.

45 The house was dark, and the man could hardly see. He lit a match and frightened the four animals. The cat scratched the man's eyes, the dog bit him on the leg, the donkey kicked the man in the stomach, and the rooster crowed loudly. The man escaped and told the leader that an evil monster 50 lived in their house. The thieves never went back to the house again.

The four animals stayed and lived happily ever after.

Did You Know?

- *The Bremen Town Musicians* was added to the second edition of *Grimm's Fairy Tales* in 1819.
- Actually, the four animals in the story never became musicians in the town of Bremen.
- The story has been adapted into other media, such as cartoons, plays, and operas.
- The stories in *Grimm's Fairy Tales* were not created by the Brothers Grimm.
- There is a statue of the four animals from the story in Bremen, Germany.

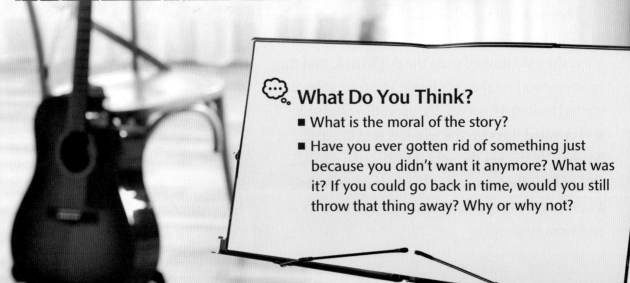

What Do You Think?

- What is the moral of the story?
- Have you ever gotten rid of something just because you didn't want it anymore? What was it? If you could go back in time, would you still throw that thing away? Why or why not?

Reading Comprehension

A. Multiple Choice

Circle the correct answer.

1 Which of the following animals is NOT part of the group?

   a. A rooster   b. A mouse

   c. A cat   d. A donkey

2 Why did the dog's master want to kill him?

   a. He could no longer hunt.

   b. He ran away.

   c. He often cried.

   d. He barked all the time.

3 What did the rooster's owner plan to do to him?

   a. Sing him a song

   b. Throw him into water

   c. Sell him to his neighbor

   d. Make him into dinner

4 Who was inside the small house when the animals walked towards it?

   a. Three musicians   b. Four thieves

   c. Five farmers   d. All of the animals' masters

5 What did the animals do to scare the thieves away?

   a. They tried to burn the house.

   b. They dressed themselves as ghosts.

   c. They sang and fell through the window.

   d. They lit matches and attacked the thieves.

B. Short Answers

Read the following questions and write down your answers.

1 What did the donkey plan to do after he ran away?

_____

2 Why couldn't the cat catch mice?

_____

3 What did the thief tell his leader about the house?

_____

Vocabulary Builder

A. Fill in the Blanks

Complete the sentences with the words and phrases below. Change the forms if necessary.

> sharp   thief   hunt   master   climb   hardly   explain   come across

1. Lions usually _____ large animals for food.

2. Leslie could _____ see the road because of the fog.

3. The dog barked happily when his _____ came home.

4. Fred was not able to _____ why he was late this morning.

5. When I was walking, I _____ a cute restaurant.

6. Timmy wasn't tall enough, so he _____ onto a chair to open the window.

7. The scissors aren't very _____, so they're OK for kids to use.

8. Catch that _____! She stole my phone!

B. Collocations of *Come*

Complete the sentences with the correct words below.

> over   along   in   across   with

1. We're going to karaoke tonight. Do you want to come _____?

2. Ian came _____ a large lake when he was went hiking.

3. The meal comes _____ a salad.

4. Edward will come _____ to our house to have dinner with us.

5. This shirt comes _____ many different colors.

Language Notes

Sense Verbs

A sense verb is a verb that describes one of the five senses: sight, sound, smell, touch, and taste.

$$S. + \begin{Bmatrix} see \\ hear \\ feel \\ smell \end{Bmatrix} + O. + \begin{Bmatrix} V. \\ V\text{-ing} \end{Bmatrix}$$

- I saw him <u>dance</u> in the park.
  ↳ to emphasize a fact
- I can hear the dog <u>barking</u>.
  ↳ to emphasize an ongoing action

$$\begin{Bmatrix} look \\ sound \\ taste \\ feel \\ smell \end{Bmatrix} + \begin{Bmatrix} like + N. \\ Adj. \end{Bmatrix}$$

- Kate's voice sounded like <u>her sister's voice</u>.
  ↳ to compare the similarity between two nouns
- The coffee tasted <u>great</u>, so I had another cup.
  ↳ to describe personal thoughts about things

Your Turn

*Complete the sentences with the **correct verbs** below. Change the forms if necessary.*

> feel taste watch look smell

❶ A good medicine _____ bitter.

❷ The perfume _____ much better than I expected.

❸ Susan _____ the sun go down yesterday.

❹ I don't _____ comfortable being here.

❺ You _____ pale. Are you all right?

READING SKILL

Making Predictions

Readers make predictions by using information they already know in order to think about what they are about to read or what will come next in the reading. This strategy helps us make connections between our own experiences and the text, which improves our memory of what we have read as well as our understanding.

Tips for making predictions:

- Look at the title first.
- Look at the pictures that go with the text.
- Based on your personal knowledge and experiences, think about what might happen next in your reading.

Test Your Skill 🎧 11

Read the following story and answer the questions.

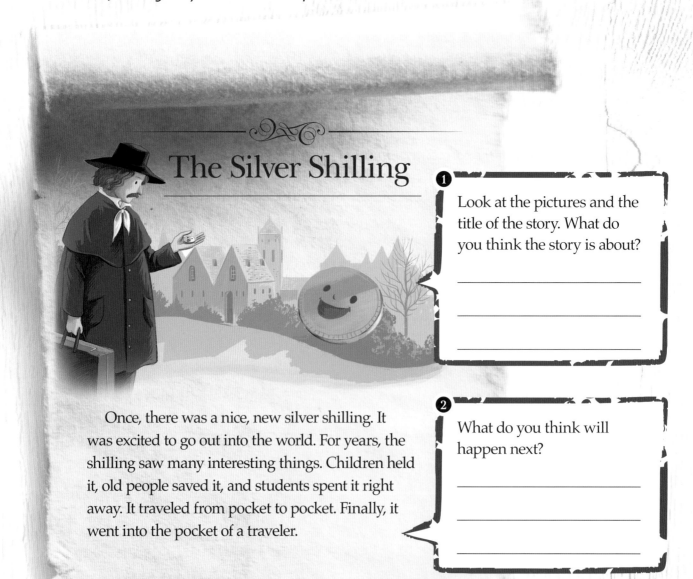

The Silver Shilling

❶ Look at the pictures and the title of the story. What do you think the story is about?

_____

_____

_____

Once, there was a nice, new silver shilling. It was excited to go out into the world. For years, the shilling saw many interesting things. Children held it, old people saved it, and students spent it right away. It traveled from pocket to pocket. Finally, it went into the pocket of a traveler.

❷ What do you think will happen next?

_____

_____

_____

The traveler brought it to a foreign country. He couldn't spend it there, so he kept it in his pocket. One day, though, it fell out and rolled away. "Now," the shilling thought, "I will see more of the world."

A man found the shilling and put it with some other coins. Then, he tried to spend them all at a shop. However, the shopkeeper would not accept the silver shilling. "This is not a real coin," he said.

In the end, the man spent the silver shilling at night in the dark. It went into a woman's purse. She was unhappy when she saw it the next day. "I can't spend this," she said. The shilling was unhappy, too. No one could use it. It felt worthless.

The woman put a hole in the shilling. "Now everyone will know this coin isn't real," she said. Still, people tried to spend it.

No one thought the shilling had value. The shilling knew that wasn't true. It kept being honest. It never pretended to be something else. Then one day, it was passed to a traveler.

The traveler recognized the shilling and brought it home. Finally, people wanted it again. It felt joy. "If you're honest and patient, everything will be OK," it thought.

③ What might the man do with the silver shilling next?

_____

_____

_____

④ What do you think might happen next?

_____

_____

_____

PUT IT IN WRITING

TASK A

*Write a 60-word paragraph about what could happen next in **The Bremen Town Musicians**.*

TASK B

Choose a novel or movie and write a review. Answer the following questions in complete sentences.

   a. What is the novel/movie about?

   b. Who are the main characters of the novel/movie?

   c. Who wrote the novel? / Who is the director of the movie?

   d. What kind of novel/movie is it (action, comedy, drama, etc.)?

   e. What do you think about the novel/movie? Is it boring, exciting, or funny?

(novel/movie name) **Review**

UNIT 4

INTERESTING LAWS AROUND THE WORLD

⊕ Learning Objectives

In this unit, you will . . .

- learn how to skim the text while reading.

> **Skimming:**
>
> *Read the text quickly to get a general understanding of the text's content.*

- learn the prefixes *il-/im-/in-/ir-*.
- learn about coordinate conjunctions.
- write about the laws or rules in your country.
- create a list of interesting facts about a country of your choice.

⏱ Get It Started

- Are there any unique rules in your country or region? What are they?

- What are some things that people do that make you feel uncomfortable? What problems do they cause?

- Do you think the actions discussed above should be illegal? Why or why not?

READING

Before Reading 🎧 12

Match the following words with their correct definitions.

❶ legal   ·   · a. someone who prepares or sells medicines

❷ maintain   ·   · b. to say officially that something is not allowed

❸ surface   ·   · c. knowing about something

❹ ban   ·   · d. the top or outside part of something

❺ army   ·   · e. allowed by law

❻ pharmacist   ·   · f. a military force that fights wars on the ground

❼ aware   ·   · g. to make a situation or activity continue in the same way

Skim the article. Then, answer the following questions.

❶ What is the overall purpose of the text?

_____

❷ Briefly explain how each paragraph is organized.

Paragraph 1: *Introduction of the topic—Some things that are illegal in one topic country might be legal in another.*

Paragraph 2: _____

Paragraph 3: _____

Paragraph 4: _____

Paragraph 5: _____

Paragraph 6: _____

fruit jelly cups

🎧 13

     Laws are different from country to country. Something that is OK and legal in one country might not be OK and illegal in another. By knowing these differences, you can understand the values of other societies. It can also help you stay out of trouble
5 when traveling.

     Take fruit jelly cups for example. Canada, the United States, and several European countries have blocked the sale of fruit jelly cups to save lives. Governments decided to ban these small snacks because their size and ingredients make

10 them a choking danger.

Environmental protection is another reason that certain products have been made illegal. To maintain its image as a clean country and to keep public spaces clean, Singapore banned the sale and import

15 of chewing gum. However, it's not illegal for tourists to have chewing gum for personal use. Another exception is a kind of gum that's used for health purposes. The people of Singapore may buy this type of gum from doctors or registered pharmacists.

chewing gum

eating and drinking

20 In Italy, it's not what you eat but where you eat that counts. Rome, Florence, and Venice have created laws that stop people from eating and drinking near ancient buildings. If you're caught eating in front of one of these buildings, you may have to pay a large

25 fine. In Venice, even the pigeons aren't safe from the law. The city has banned pigeon feeding as a way to lower the population of these birds. Pigeons build nests on top of structures and ruin surfaces with their claws and droppings.

pigeons

army colored clothes

bikini / swimming trunks

30   There are also laws to do with clothing that you should be aware of. In Barbados, it's illegal to wear army-colored clothing since this style is only for the country's defense force. In Barcelona, it's illegal to wear a bikini or swimming trunks outside of beach areas.

35   While such laws may seem strange to us, they do make sense in other countries. Therefore, be aware of other countries' laws, and you'll find a deeper understanding of their cultures as well.

Did You Know?

- It's illegal to climb a tree in Oshawa, Ontario, Canada.

- In Baltimore, Maryland, you're banned from taking your pet lion to the movie theater.

- You'll be fined if you run out of gas on the autobahn in Germany.

- In Victoria, Canada, it's illegal for two bagpipers to perform at the same time.

 What Do You Think?

■ Do you agree with any of the laws mentioned in the passage? Why or why not?

■ What do you think should be made illegal in your country or region? Why?

Reading Comprehension

A. True or False

*Read the statements below and write **T** for true or **F** for false.*

_____ ❶ Laws are pretty similar between different countries.

_____ ❷ You can't sell chewing gum in Singapore.

_____ ❸ It is illegal to eat outside in Italy.

_____ ❹ Only the country's defense force can wear army colored clothing in Barbados.

B. Short Answers

Read the following questions and write down your answers.

❶ Why are fruit jelly cups banned in Canada?

_____

❷ What can you NOT do in Rome, Florence, and Venice?

_____

❸ How is Venice dealing with its pigeon problem?

_____

❹ Where is it illegal to wear a bikini or swimming trunks outside of the beach?

_____

C. Identify Referents

Check what the following words in bold refer to.

❶ **them** (paragraph 2, line 10)
  ☐ fruit jelly cups   ☐ governments   ☐ human lives

❷ **its** (paragraph 3, line 13)
  ☐ Singapore's   ☐ enviromental protection's   ☐ the public's

❸ **their** (paragraph 4, line 28)
  ☐ the structures'   ☐ the pigeons'   ☐ the nests'

Vocabulary Builder

A. Fill in the Blanks

Complete the sentences with the words and phrases below. Change the forms if necessary.

fine	ruin	danger	ingredient
block	make sense	against	strange

❶ Our dinner was _____ after I burnt the chicken.

❷ Fires are a big source of _____ during the summer.

❸ Shannon's story is _____, but it's true.

❹ Emily has fought _____ laws that she doesn't agree with.

❺ The police officer gave me a(n) _____ for driving too fast.

❻ Combine all the _____ in a large bowl.

❼ I think his plan to leave early for the airport _____.

❽ The government has _____ the import of some foreign-made products.

B. Prefixes: *il-/im-/in-/ir-*

The prefixes il-, im-, in-, ir- are usually used to present negative meaning. Look at the following examples. Then, complete the sentences with the correct form of words.

- il + legal = illegal
- im + possible = impossible
- in + correct = incorrect
- ir + regular = irregular

❶ The _____ work schedule makes it difficult for us to plan in advance. (regular)

❷ Ken's answer is _____. He got the wrong answer. (correct)

❸ That loud noise makes it _____ to sleep. (possible)

❹ Driving over the speed limit on the highway is _____. (legal)

48

Language Notes

Coordinate Conjunctions

A and/or/but B

and: to join similar ideas

- <u>Tim</u> and <u>Doris</u> are my friends.
  ↘ to connect words

- John <u>cooked dinner</u> and <u>cleaned the house</u> this evening.
  ↘ to connect phrases

....

or: to show a necessary choice

- Which do you want, <u>coffee</u> or <u>tea</u>?
  to connect words ↙

- Do you want to <u>watch a movie</u> or <u>go jogging</u>?
  to connect phrases

....

but: to show differences

- These shoes are <u>old</u> but <u>comfortable</u>.
  to connect words ↙

- This tool is <u>easy to use</u> but <u>difficult to carry around</u>.
  ↘ to connect phrases

Your Turn

Fill in the blanks using the conjunctions: and, or, or but.

❶ Do you want to stay here _____ go home?

❷ I'll invite both Bobby _____ Alice to my birthday party.

❸ I like most seasons, _____ not summer.

❹ Tim is a vegetarian. He doesn't eat meat _____ fish.

❺ It's an old car, _____ it's very reliable.

❻ Luke didn't speak to anyone _____ nobody spoke to him.

READING SKILL

Skimming

When we skim a text, we read it quickly to gain a general understanding of the text's content. By skimming, we can get the following information:

- The general topic and purpose of a text
- The organization of the text
- The perspective or viewpoint of the writer

Tips for skimming:

- Read at about three to four times your normal reading speed.
- Do not read each word. Instead, search for "keywords."

Test Your Skill 🎧 14

Skim the following passage and answer the questions below.

This semester, I moved to Seoul, Korea as an exchange student. Everything here is new to me, and I find the culture so much different from my hometown in Canada.

Age is very important in Korean culture. When Korean people meet each other for the first time, they often ask each other, "How old are you?" This is because they need to know who is older in order to use the proper language. In Korea, elders are highly respected. Younger family members are responsible for caring for their aging family members. For example, they set the table and ask their elders to eat first.

Korean food culture is another difference. Sharing food is common here as people think sharing is caring. When I dined with my Korean friends at a restaurant, we shared all the food in front of us. It's nice that I got to taste other kinds of dishes!

❶ What is the topic of this passage?

_____

❷ What are the main ideas for paragraph 2 and 3?

Paragraph 2: _____

Paragraph 3: _____

PUT IT IN WRITING

TASK A

Write a short message to a friend who is visiting your country. Tell him or her about any laws or rules that are important to know about.

Welcome to LiveChat   — ▢ ✕

👤 _____ *(your friend)*

> Is there anything I need to know before visiting your country? 😟

🔊 ☺ 📎

....
....
....
....
....

TASK B

Work in pairs. Choose a country and write four interesting facts about it. Have these facts changed your opinion of it? Share your thoughts with the class.

Country: Japan

In Japan, there is a unique job called a "passenger pusher." These people help push passengers onto a crowded train.

Country:

❶ ....

❷ ....

❸ ....

❹ ....

UNIT 5

THE OLYMPIC GAMES: A HISTORY OF FIRSTS

⊕ Learning Objectives

In this unit, you will ...

- learn to identify time order of events in a text.

> **Understanding time order:**
> *Read the text and look for the order in which events take place.*

- learn the suffix *-al*.
- learn about conjunctive adverbs.
- write about a baseball player's day.
- create a timeline of important events for a sport or a sports player.

⏱ Get It Started

The following are some Olympic events. Match the words to the correct pictures.

judo
boxing
gymnastics
fencing
table tennis
sailing

53

Before Reading 🎧 CD 15

Match the following words and phrases with their correct definitions.

❶ spread　·

❷ take part　·

❸ represent　·

❹ individual　·

❺ flame　·

❻ competition　·

❼ tune in　·

· a. intended for one person rather than a group

· b. an event in which people compete with each other

· c. to do an activity with other people

· d. to watch or listen to a broadcast on television or radio

· e. a stream of hot, burning gas from something on fire

· f. to cover a wider area

· g. to officially speak or take action for another person or group of people

Scan the article. Then, match the event to the year on the timeline.

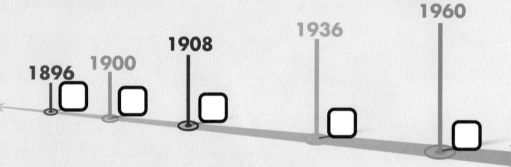

1896　**1900**　**1908**　**1936**　**1960**

a.　The entire world could watch the Olympics on TV.

b.　People from Berlin were able to see the Olympics on large screens.

c.　Soccer was introduced as the first team game at the Olympics.

d.　The first modern Olympic Games started.

e.　Athletes started to compete for their own countries.

🎧 CD 16

People line the street to watch the flame pass by. A woman jogs with a torch held high. She comes to a stop and lights the torch of another jogger. Soon afterwards, in the dark,
5 from the center of a stadium, an archer shoots

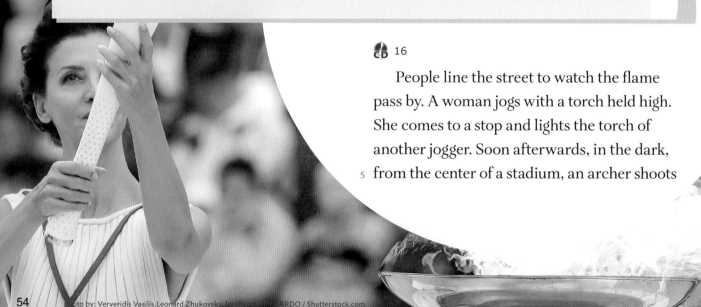

the flame into a cauldron. This is part of the Olympics—the biggest international sports event. The Olympics has a rich history which includes a lot of "firsts." Here's a look back at some of the times when the Olympics
10 broke new ground. Let's begin at the beginning.

The first recorded Olympic Games were held around 776 BC in the city of Olympia, Greece. The purpose of the ancient games was to honor the Greek god Zeus. In the beginning, running was the only sports event. Later, more events were included, such as boxing and horse racing. During
15 this period, only Greek males could take part in the games. However, the ancient games came to an end with the fall of the Greek Empire.

Centuries later, the games were brought back. In 1896 in Athens, the first modern Olympic Games began. At this time, more events were added. Male athletes from different countries joined the games, too. Four years
20 later, in Paris, female athletes entered the Olympics for the first time.

The ancient games were meant to celebrate individual greatness. Thus, team competitions came along only much later. The first team game introduced was soccer in 1900. At this time, soccer matches were played between clubs from different countries. Then, in 1908, individual and
25 team competitors began representing their own countries. That year, to start off the Olympics, athletes walked proudly into the stadium in London behind their national flags. In addition, a swimming pool was used for the first time.

The excitement of watching the Olympic
30 Games began to spread in 1936. The Olympics
were hosted in Berlin that year, and the event was
shown on large screens across the city. In 1948,
the London Games aired on TV in homes across
Britain. Finally, in 1960, the whole world could
35 catch the Olympics in Rome on TV.

Every four years, sports fans tune in to see if more
Olympic firsts can be achieved. The Olympic tradition
lives on, and it continues to give us a lot of fun.

Did You Know?

- During the ancient Olympics, males didn't wear any clothes in the games.
- At the first modern Olympic Games in 1896, the winner received a silver medal instead of a gold one.
- In fact, Olympic gold medals are made mostly from silver.
- The Olympic rings represent the union of the five continents: Europe, Asia, Africa, America, and Australia.

What Do You Think?

■ How do the Olympic Games influence our lives?
■ What are the positive and negative sides to hosting the Olympic Games?

Reading Comprehension

A. True or False

*Read the statements below and write **T** for true or **F** for false.*

_____ ❶ Horse racing was introduced to the Olympics in 1896.

_____ ❷ Female athletes joined the Olympics for the first time in 1900.

_____ ❸ Team competitions came earlier than individual competitions.

_____ ❹ The first time a swimming pool was used in the Olympics was in 1936.

_____ ❺ People in Britain were not able to watch the Olympics on TV until 1948.

B. Short Answers

Read the following questions and write down your answers.

❶ When did the first ancient Olympic Games take place?

_____

❷ Why were the ancient Olympic Games held?

_____

❸ In which city did female athletes join the Olympics for the first time?

_____

❹ What was the first team game that was introduced in the Olympics?

_____

C. Identify Referents

Check what the following words in bold refer to.

❶ **which** (paragraph 1, line 8)

☐ the flame   ☐ the Olympics' history   ☐ the stadium

❷ **their** (paragraph 4, line 27)

☐ the athletes'   ☐ the clubs'   ☐ the different countries'

Vocabulary Builder

A. Fill in the Blanks

Complete the sentences with the words below. Change the forms if necessary.

> light purpose host match achieve ancient tradition international

❶ The final score of the _____ was two to nothing.

❷ It's pretty cold, so we should _____ a fire to keep warm.

❸ Giving red envelopes is a Chinese New Year _____.

❹ The _____ of my trip was to learn Chinese.

❺ Billy works hard to _____ his goals.

❻ In _____ times, people used the sun to tell time.

❼ I'm going to _____ a party this weekend, and you're invited.

❽ English is a(n) _____ language. It is spoken around the world.

B. Suffix: -al

The suffix -al is often added to a noun to make an adjective. Look at the following examples. Then, complete the sentences with the correct form of words.

- national
- traditional
- educational
- personal

❶ The maple is the _____ tree of Canada. (nation)

❷ Vivian seldom talks about her _____ life. (person)

❸ Please list your _____ qualifications and work experience. (education)

❹ The dancers in the show wore _____ clothes. (tradition)

Language Notes

Conjunctive Adverbs

Usage	Conjunctions
contrast	however, nevertheless, nonetheless
cause and effect	therefore, hence, thus
additional information	besides, also, in addition, furthermore

$$S. + V. + \begin{Bmatrix} . \\ ; \end{Bmatrix} + \textbf{conjunctive adverb,} + S. + V.$$

- I don't have any free time this week. However, I'm free next week.

  contrast

  = I don't have any free time this week. I'm free next week, **however.**

- Nick had a cold; therefore, he stayed home yesterday.

  cause   effect

- The shoes don't fit me. Besides, they're too expensive.

  additional information

Your Turn

Read the following sentences and circle the correct answers.

❶ Andy wanted to call Rose. (However / Hence), he didn't have her phone number.

❷ The meal comes with soup. (Besides / Therefore), you get your choice of dessert.

❸ I overslept; (thus / nevertheless), I was late for school.

❹ The house is beautiful. (Furthermore / However), it's in a great location.

❺ The village was extremely beautiful. (Therefore / Nonetheless), Meg couldn't imagine spending the rest of her life there.

59

READING SKILL

Understanding Time Order

In some reading texts like biographies or stories, events are described based on time order. Identifying the year, month, week, day, or hour is a useful tip to understand time order. Another tip is to look for clue words. Here are some examples:

first, in the beginning, next, then, before, soon after, a few years later, ever since, until, by the time, previously, immediately, shortly

Test Your Skill 🎧 17

Read the following story about Beethoven. Then, put the events in order.

Ludwig van Beethoven was born in Germany in 1770. His father was a musician, and he wanted his son to become a musician, too. When Beethoven was just five years old, his father started giving him piano lessons. Later, family friends taught him the violin and the organ. By the time Beethoven was seven years old, everyone could see that he was a musical genius. He started holding concerts to provide his family with income.

Beethoven was often ill, and that affected his hearing. He was deaf by the time he turned 40. This stopped him from playing music, but not from writing it. He could still "hear" each note in his head. Beethoven conducted his Ninth Symphony at a concert after he became deaf. Everyone loved it. They clapped and cheered, but Beethoven couldn't hear them. Someone had to turn Beethoven around to see all of the excited people. Beethoven's music was the most exciting music at that time. It's still popular today.

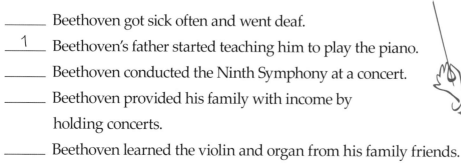

_____ Beethoven got sick often and went deaf.

___1___ Beethoven's father started teaching him to play the piano.

_____ Beethoven conducted the Ninth Symphony at a concert.

_____ Beethoven provided his family with income by holding concerts.

_____ Beethoven learned the violin and organ from his family friends.

PUT IT IN WRITING

TASK A

Look at the following pictures and write a 50-word paragraph about what Andy does in a day.

TASK B

Work in pairs. Choose a sport or a sports player and add some important events to the timeline.
Then, share your findings with the class.

UNIT 6

RECIPES TO PARTY WITH

⊕ Learning Objectives

In this unit, you will . . .

- learn to follow explicit instructions in a text.

> **Following explicit instructions:**
>
> *Read the text carefully to understand the directions.*

- learn some common measure words.
- learn to use imperatives.
- write a recipe.
- create a food diary entry.

⏱ Get It Started

Look up the following kitchen verbs in a dictionary. Then, match the words to the correct pictures.

chop
stir
peel
crack
spread
pour

Before Reading 🎧 18

Match the following words with their correct definitions.

❶ serve • • a. a large cup with straight sides used for hot drinks

❷ lid • • b. to take something away from a place

❸ remove • • c. calmly or softly

❹ gently • • d. a cover on a container

❺ recipe • • e. a type of food that is eaten in addition to your usual meals

❻ treat • • f. to provide food or drinks

❼ mug • • g. a set of instructions telling you how to prepare and cook food

Scan the passage. Then, connect the ingredients to the recipes.

flour   milk   fruit   corn kernels   pineapple juice   egg   salt   butter

🎧 19

Are you looking for something to serve at a party? Look no further! Below, we have a mug cake, popcorn, and fruit punch recipe just for you. These popular treats are quick and easy to make. With just a couple of steps, you can make them yourself. Why don't you give them a try?

mug cake

Mug Cake

Things You Will Need:

- 4 tbsp cake flour
- 3 tbsp milk
- Pinch of salt

- 2 tbsp cocoa powder
- 3 tbsp vegetable oil
- Mug

tablespoon
- 4 <u>tbsp</u> sugar
- 1 egg
- Microwave

Steps:

1. Put the flour, cocoa powder, sugar, and a pinch of salt into the mug. Mix them well.
2. Mix in the milk and vegetable oil.
3. Crack the egg into the mug. Stir everything together.
4. Put the mug into the microwave. Heat it for two minutes.
5. Take the mug out of the microwave and let it cool down for two minutes.
6. Enjoy your mug cake!

Popcorn

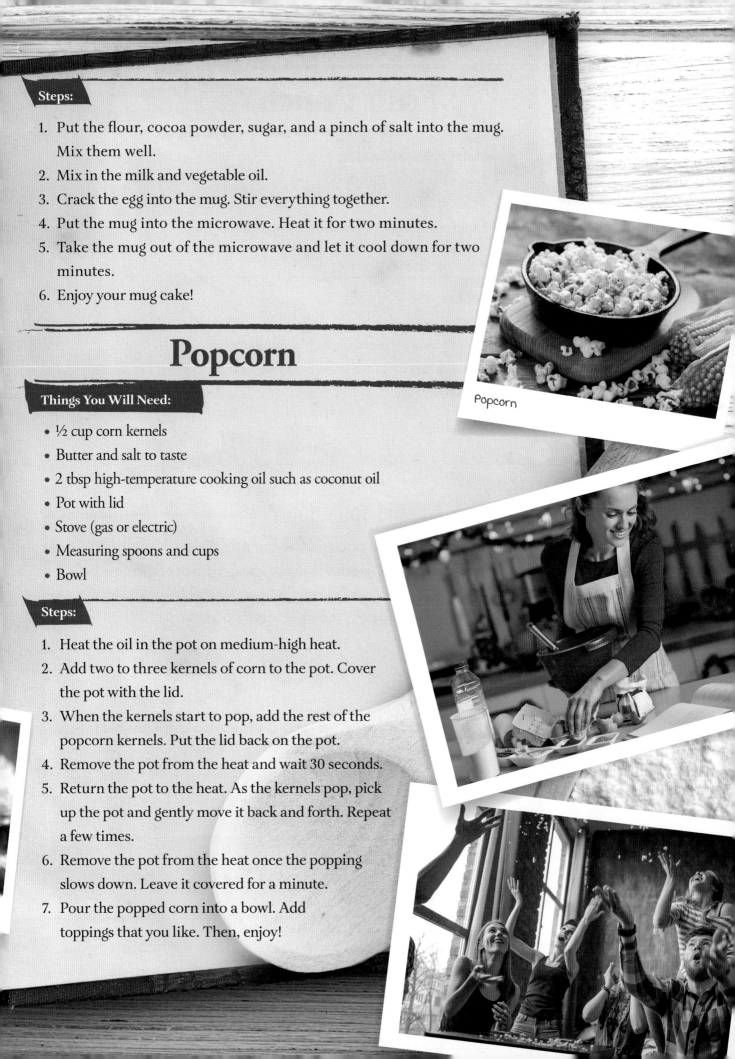

Popcorn

Things You Will Need:

- ½ cup corn kernels
- Butter and salt to taste
- 2 tbsp high-temperature cooking oil such as coconut oil
- Pot with lid
- Stove (gas or electric)
- Measuring spoons and cups
- Bowl

Steps:

1. Heat the oil in the pot on medium-high heat.
2. Add two to three kernels of corn to the pot. Cover the pot with the lid.
3. When the kernels start to pop, add the rest of the popcorn kernels. Put the lid back on the pot.
4. Remove the pot from the heat and wait 30 seconds.
5. Return the pot to the heat. As the kernels pop, pick up the pot and gently move it back and forth. Repeat a few times.
6. Remove the pot from the heat once the popping slows down. Leave it covered for a minute.
7. Pour the popped corn into a bowl. Add toppings that you like. Then, enjoy!

Fruit Punch

Things You Will Need:

- 8 cups Hawaiian Punch
- 4 cups ginger ale
- Large punch bowl or pitcher
- Ice
- 1.5 cups pineapple juice
- Any fruit you like
- Large spoon

Steps:

1. Slice the fruit.
2. Gently mix all ingredients in a punch bowl or pitcher.
3. Serve over ice.

Fruit Punch

Did You Know?

- Mug cakes can be made in five minutes or less.
- Popcorn has been served in movie theaters in the U.S. since 1912.
- Popped popcorn comes in two shapes: butterfly and mushroom. Mushroom popcorn is round. Butterfly popcorn has little "wings."

mushroom

butterfly

- Water inside a corn kernel turns into steam when it heats up. The steam's pressure pops the kernel and turns it inside out.
- Punch can be made with or without alcohol.
- It is believed that punch was introduced to the U.K. by Indian sailors in the early 17th century.

💭 What Do You Think?

- What do you think of your skills as a cook? Share your cooking experiences if you have any.
- If you were to have a party, what foods would you prepare? What would the party be like?

Reading Comprehension

A. Multiple Choice

Circle the correct answer.

1 According to the recipe, how much milk is needed to make a mug cake?

   a. One tablespoon   b. Two tablespoons

   c. Three tablespoons   d. Four tablespoons

2 To make a mug cake, what's the next step after mixing everything together?

   a. Let the cake cool down

   b. Add some vegetable oil

   c. Microwave for two minutes

   d. Enjoy the mug cake

3 What is NOT included in the popcorn recipe?

   a. Salt   b. Corn kernels

   c. Butter   d. Cocoa powder

4 How long should you cover the pot before pouring the popped corn into a bowl?

   a. Ten seconds   b. Thirty seconds

   c. One minute   d. Ten minutes

5 What is true about the fruit punch recipe?

   a. You can add any type of fruit to the punch.

   b. You will need a large fork and a pitcher.

   c. You should heat the juice before serving.

   d. It takes more than five steps to make it.

B. Short Answers

Read the following questions and write down your answers.

1 How much salt is needed for the mug cake recipe?

_____

2 What temperature should the stove be on to heat the oil for making popcorn?

_____

3 What ingredients do we need for the fruit punch recipe?

_____

Vocabulary Builder

A. Fill in the Blanks

Complete the sentences with the words and phrases below. Change the forms if necessary.

> mix   stove   slice   cool down   treat   step   powder   give it a try

❶ For the next _____, add some garlic to the pan.

❷ This noodle dish is too hot. I'll eat it after it _____.

❸ Gina turned on the _____ to boil water.

❹ I made an apple pie. You should _____.

❺ The white _____ on the cake is sugar.

❻ The loaf of bread was _____ into 20 pieces.

❼ If you _____ blue and yellow, you get green.

❽ The candy shop has all kinds of tasty _____.

B. Measure Words

Look at the pictures and fill in the blanks with the words below.

> ◎ cup   piece   cube   loaf   glass   jar   pinch   tablespoon

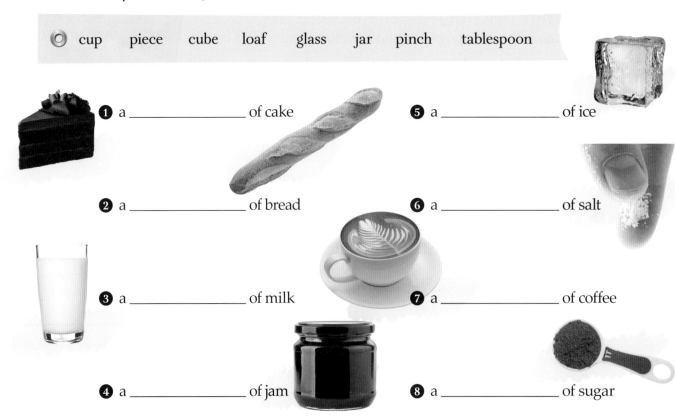

❶ a _____ of cake

❷ a _____ of bread

❸ a _____ of milk

❹ a _____ of jam

❺ a _____ of ice

❻ a _____ of salt

❼ a _____ of coffee

❽ a _____ of sugar

Language Notes

Imperatives

(Don't +) base verb (+ O.)

- Heat the cake for two minutes.
  ↘ to suggest
- Don't bring your pets in.
  ↘ to command

(Don't +) be + { Adj. / N. }

- Be quiet, <u>please</u>. = Please be quiet.
  ↘ to make it sound more polite
- Don't be a fool.

Your Turn

*Fill in the blanks with **imperatives** using the hints.*

❶ It's cold outside. _____ to bring your coat with you. (not forget)

❷ _____ . There are so many cars on the street. (careful)

❸ _____ early, or you'll be late for school. (go to bed)

❹ _____ . I'm on your side. (not worry)

❺ Please _____ and wait for your turn. (patient)

READING SKILL

Following Explicit Instructions

Explicit content is often found in texts that give clear instructions (e.g., how-to guides) and commands (e.g., swimming pool rules). Although explicit information may seem easier to understand than implicit (i.e., "hidden") information, it actually requires more skill to keep the information in mind. To follow explicit instructions, it's important to pay attention to the details.

Test Your Skill   CD 20

Read the following toaster oven instructions. Then, read the statements below and write T for true or F for false.

How to Use

① Plug the power cord into the outlet.

② Preheat the oven to the desired temperature.

③ Open the oven door and put the food on the metal oven rack.

   * The oven rack should always be in place when baking.

④ Close the oven door.

⑤ Turn the timer knob to the desired bake time.

⑥ When the timer goes off, take your food out of the oven.

   * The oven will automatically turn off when the timer reaches zero.

⑦ Unplug the power cord.

_____ ❶ The oven needs batteries for power.

_____ ❷ You should heat the oven before putting food inside.

_____ ❸ To use the oven, you should place the food on the oven rack.

_____ ❹ To bake, you must press the timer button.

_____ ❺ The oven will stop running 30 seconds after the timer reaches zero.

PUT IT IN WRITING

TASK A

Choose a food or drink that you want to make. Create a recipe with clear instructions.

Recipe:

Things you will need:

Steps:

TASK B

Write a food diary entry below. Then, find out your daily calorie needs online. What do you think about your diet? Share your thoughts with the class.

Meal	Food/Drink	Calories
Breakfast		
Lunch		
Dinner		
Snack		
Total		

Amount of water I drank:
(each cup = 500 ml)

Part A 🎧 21

There was once an old man. He was very rich, __(1)__ he never used any of his wealth. Instead, he kept __(2)__ his gold coins in a case. He buried the case in a secret spot in his garden.

Each day, the man went into his garden. He dug up the case and opened it. __(3)__, he counted the coins one by one.

After the man counted the last coin, he shut the case and buried his treasure once more. The next day, he did this all over again.

One night, someone took the coins. When the man came and saw the empty hole, he went wild with anger. A traveler heard and asked what was wrong. "Someone robbed me! My __(4)__ gold is gone!" yelled the man.

"Why was your gold in that hole? If it's there, you can't spend it," said the traveler. The man said, "I would __(5)__ spend my gold!"

The traveler threw a stone into the hole. "Bury this, then," he said. "It's worth just as much ..."

A. *Choose the best answers to complete the text.*

_____ ❶ a. or   b. then
          c. but   d. also

_____ ❷ a. all of   b. none of
          c. little of   d. little

_____ ❸ a. Finally   b. For example
          c. However   d. Then

_____ ❹ a. precious   b. public
          c. peaceful   d. possible

_____ **5** a. ever   b. never

                c. often   d. always

B. _Read the passage again and answer the following questions._

_____ **1** Where did the rich man keep his gold coins?

         a. In his pocket   b. In a neighbor's garden

         c. In a case   d. In a nest

_____ **2** What did the rich man do each day?

         a. He added new coins to the case.

         b. He counted his gold coins.

         c. He visited a new secret spot.

         d. He watered his garden.

_____ **3** What happened when the rich man found that his money was gone?

         a. He was really mad.   b. He cried very hard.

         c. He robbed the other guy.   d. He dug another hole.

_____ **4** What did the traveler throw into the hole?

         a. A stone   b. A coin

         c. Some silver   d. A case

_____ **5** What will the traveler most likely say next after "It's worth just as much …"?

         a. Money will be worth more if you save it.

         b. Keep most of your money in a safe place.

         c. Count the amount of money you have every day.

         d. Wealth has no value if it's never used.

_____ **6** Which of the following is true about this story?

         a. The traveler gave the gold coins to the poor.

         b. The rich man sold his coins to the traveler.

         c. The traveler kept all of his treasure in a secret hole.

         d. The rich man buried his gold coins in his garden.

Belize: The Land of Adventure

Belize is a tiny country in Central America which sits between Guatemala and the Caribbean Sea. If you are into sun, sand, and adventures, then Belize is the place for you!

Belize is popular __(1)__ international visitors. Most go to enjoy its sunny weather, beautiful beaches, and clear blue waters. People __(2)__ see whale sharks, sea turtles, and so much more under the water.

For water lovers, there are several activites to choose __(3)__. Why not swim around the Belize Barrier Reef—the second largest reef in the world? It has over 100 kinds of coral, plus 500 types of fish. People also can't get enough of the Great Blue Hole. At over 400 feet deep, it's the world's largest sinkhole.

Belize isn't just about water activities. On land, people can __(4)__ its many national parks and get close to nature. They can see animals from ants to monkeys to jaguars. Also, around 570 types of birds make their nests in the jungles of Belize.

The country is home to many ancient Mayan ruins, too. They include giant stone temples with walls of steps. From the top, visitors can __(5)__ the views that kings once enjoyed. Belize has so much more. If you plan on visiting, don't limit your adventures to what's in the travel guides.

A. *Choose the best answers to complete the text.*

_____ **❶** a. about b. with
c. on d. by

_____ **❷** a. can b. does
c. are d. have

_____ **❸** a. from b. upon
c. into d. above

_____ **❹** a. pray b. hunt
c. hold d. visit

74

_____ ❺ a. reach out   b. speak out
        c. check out   d. watch out

B. *Read the passage again and answer the following questions.*

_____ ❶ Where is Belize located?
        a. In Europe   b. In Central America
        c. In Africa   d. In Asia

_____ ❷ What is Belize NOT known for?
        a. Sunny weather   b. Clear blue waters
        c. Pretty beaches   d. Snowy views

_____ ❸ What is true about the Belize Barrier Reef?
        a. It is the largest reef in the world.
        b. It is home to around 50 kinds of coral.
        c. There are 500 kinds of fish.
        d. It is under 400 feet deep.

_____ ❹ What is the main idea of the fourth paragraph?
        a. On-land activities in Belize
        b. The number of birds in Belize
        c. Introduction of the Great Blue Hole
        d. International visitors in Belize

_____ ❺ Which ancient ruins can you find in Belize?
        a. Ancient Aztec ruins   b. Ancient Mayan ruins
        c. Ancient Egyptian ruins   d. Ancient Indian ruins

_____ ❻ What does the author think about traveling in Belize?
        a. Travel guides don't list everything you can see and do in Belize.
        b. Never travel alone, as Belize is a dangerous place.
        c. The first thing to do is to see every kind of bird there.
        d. There aren't many activities to do there, but it's a nice place to relax.

C. *Scan the passage and underline the topic sentence for each paragraph.*

Summer Beach Safety

⚠ **Check the weather in advance.**
Never go to the beach in bad weather. If you see lightning, get __(1)__ the water right away.

⚠ **Beware of waves.**
Waves are more powerful than you think. They can __(2)__ injuries or even death.

⚠ **Never swim alone.**
Never swim alone, even if you're a good swimmer. Make sure a lifeguard can always see you.

⚠ **Avoid sunburn.**
Wear a hat, sunglasses, __(3)__ sunscreen. Also, use a beach umbrella to __(4)__ your skin.

⚠ **Read the warning signs.**
Some beaches have important warning signs. __(5)__ obey them.

⚠ **Don't drink alcohol.**
Alcohol affects your judgment. Don't drink before you go swimming.

A. *Choose the best answers to complete the text.*

_____ ❶ a. into   b. from
c. up   d. out of

_____ ❷ a. result   b. rise
c. lead   d. cause

_____ ❸ a. and   b. but
c. besides   d. so

_____ ❹ a. damage   b. spread

c. protect   d. heat

_____ ❺ a. Be sure to   b. Being sure to

c. Be sure   d. Sure to

B. Read the passage again and answer the following questions.

_____ ❶ For summer beach safety, what should we do about the weather?

a. Go to the beach right after it rains.

b. Check the weather report before we go to the beach.

c. Stay in the water if we see lightning.

d. Stay under a tree when it's hot.

_____ ❷ The phrase "beware of" in point 2, is closest in meaning to "_____."

a. stay away from   b. take care of

c. be careful of   d. take a look at

_____ ❸ What is suggested about swimming?

a. Be a good swimmer.   b. Become a lifeguard.

c. Do not swim by yourself.   d. Never swim too fast.

_____ ❹ Which of the following is NOT a tip to avoid sunburn?

a. Apply sunscreen.   b. Wear sunglasses.

c. Use a beach umbrella.   d. Put on a swimsuit.

_____ ❺ What is true about beach warning signs?

a. You need to make sure you follow them.

b. You can't find many of them at the beach.

c. You can check the weather with them.

d. They're usually located next to a beach umbrella.

_____ ❻ Why shouldn't we drink alcohol before going swimming?

a. We will have a fever.

b. We might not be able to think clearly.

c. It's really bad for our skin.

d. We will attract wild animals.

The Birth of the
Hamburger

Did you know that the history of the hamburger is much longer than the history of the U.S.? In the 13th century, Mongol soldiers would put meat under their saddles. This was to make the meat softer __(1)__ easier to eat. The Mongols brought this dish to Russia. There, it became a favorite dish and is known today as steak tartare. This is raw ground beef __(2)__ a raw egg.

By the 17th century, Russians had brought steak tartare to the port of Hamburg, Germany. The locals there had the idea to cook it. This dish became known __(3)__ Hamburg steak. By the mid-1800s, people from Hamburg came to the U.S. with this popular local dish. In 1891, an American named Oscar Weber Bilby __(4)__ a Fourth of July party at his cow farm. He grilled patties of ground beef and put them on buns. The modern hamburger was born.

The world's first burger chain, White Castle, opened in 1921. It became famous __(5)__ its little square burgers, which sold for just five cents. In 1940 McDonald's opened. Today, Americans eat about 50 billion burgers a year. Now, the hamburger can be found all over the world. Wherever you are, you can just get a burger, and you're good to go!

Reading Comprehension

A. *Choose the best answers to complete the text.*

_____ ❶ a. but   b. and
         c. or   d. so

_____ ❷ a. with   b. as
         c. to   d. of

_____ ❸ a. to   b. from
         c. as   d. with

_____ ❹ a. took   b. owned
         c. held   d. got

_____ **5** a. to   b. on

       c. as   d. for

B. _Scan the passage and put the events in order._

_____ Russians brought steak tartare to the port of Hamburg.

_____ Oscar Weber Bilby put grilled beef on buns.

___1___ Mongol soldiers put meat under their saddles.

_____ The first burger chain opened.

_____ People from Hamburg brought Hamburg steak to the U.S.

_____ A dish from the Mongols was brought to Russia.

C. _Read the passage again and write **T** for true or **F** for false._

_____ **1** The history of the U.S. is shorter than that of the hamburger.

_____ **2** Mongol soldiers invented a dish called Hamburg steak.

_____ **3** McDonald's was the world's first burger chain.

_____ **4** In 1921, square burgers sold for just five cents.

_____ **5** Americans eat five billion burgers a year nowadays.

D. _Read the following questions and write down your answers._

1 What is the overall purpose of the text?

_____

2 Why did the Mongol fighters put meat under their saddles?

_____

3 What is steak tartare?

_____

4 Who made the first modern burger?

_____

79

UNIT 7

DANCING IN THE STREETZ: HOUSE OF HOP

⊕ Learning Objectives

In this unit, you will . . .

- learn how to visualize text while reading.

> **Visualizing text:**
>
> *Read the text and create a mental picture based on what you read.*

- learn multiple usages of words found within the passage.
- learn about infinitives.
- answer questions about a flyer.
- describe a painting.

⏱ Get It Started

- Do you like to dance? Why or why not?
- Research the following dance styles. What is special about each one?

locking

voguing

jazz

popping

house

breaking

READING

Before Reading  25

Match the following words and phrases with their correct definitions.

❶ impress ·

❷ look forward to ·

❸ forehead ·

❹ contract ·

❺ common ·

❻ rotate ·

❼ involve ·

· a. to make something become shorter or smaller in size

· b. to cause someone to admire you

· c. the same in a lot of places or for a lot of people

· d. to feel excited about something that is going to happen

· e. to include something

· f. to cause something to turn in a circle

· g. the flat part of the face, above the eyes and below the hair

Read the following passage. Then, draw your mental picture in the space provided.

The kick-out is a simple step you can use to impress your friends. First, go into a squat position with your weight on the balls of your feet. Place your left hand beside your left hip on the floor. Then, kick your left leg out.

26

Welcome to Streetz: House of Hop. We have been teaching street dance since 1991. Our teachers are excited to bring you the very best of house, b-boying/b-girling, popping,
5 and locking. See our schedule below. We look forward to dancing with you soon!

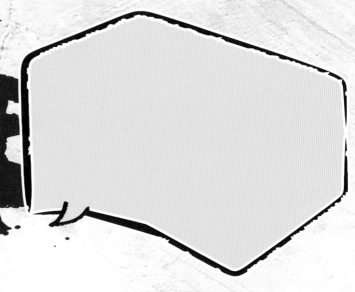

House

This rule-free street dance started in the underground clubs of New York and Chicago. It began in the late 1970s and early 1980s. Dancers use fast footwork and fluid body movements in
10 this style. Get in the groove with a sample below.

Troy

Mon. 6:30 p.m.–7:30 p.m.

Wed. 8:00 p.m.–9:00 p.m.

Jacking is one of the basic movements of house. To do the jack, start with your feet hip-width apart. Bend your knees a little bit, bring your hips forward and come straight up. Try to roll your body so your chest moves forward and out with your head dropping back. With practice, your body will flow with the movement.

B-Boying/B-Girling

This style was developed in New York during the 1970s. It involves footwork, movements on the floor, freezing in a movement, and acrobatic power moves. Try the energetic move below!

Estella

Tue. 7:30 p.m.–8:30 p.m.

Sat. 10:00 a.m.–11:00 a.m.

The kick-out is a simple step to impress your friends. First, go into a squat position with your weight on the balls of your feet. Place your left hand beside your left hip on the floor. Then, kick your left leg out. For added style, place your right hand against your forehead. Bring your right leg back and repeat on your left side.

Popping

This style comes from LA. To pop, you must contract a desired muscle group to the beat of the music. Pop onto the scene with the following dance.

Jackson

Mon. 7:30 p.m.–8:30 p.m.

Thurs. 7:00 p.m.–8:00 p.m.

83

30   Chest popping is a popular move. To start, arch your lower back and tighten your upper back. Try to imagine hitting the ceiling with your chest. Add the pop by contracting your upper back quickly.

Locking

    Like popping, locking comes from LA. It involves going from
35 a fast movement to freezing in a position for a moment and then going back to the original speed. Twirl to the music with the move below.

    The wrist twirl is a basic locking move found in many dancers' bags of tricks. Bring your arm up to your shoulder with
40 your elbow bent. At the same time, make a big circle with your wrist. Once you can't go any further, stop and rotate your wrist back to the start.

Pauline

Fri. 8:00 p.m.–9:00 p.m.

Sat. 4:00 p.m.–5:00 p.m.

    Not sure which class to try? Take advantage of our New Year's open house from January 1 to 8. Then, register for a semester or take drop-in classes. The choice is yours. What are you waiting for?

Did You Know?

- Hip hop is a cultural and art movement that was created in New York City. It includes DJing, rap, graffiti, and dance.
- Common street dance clothing:

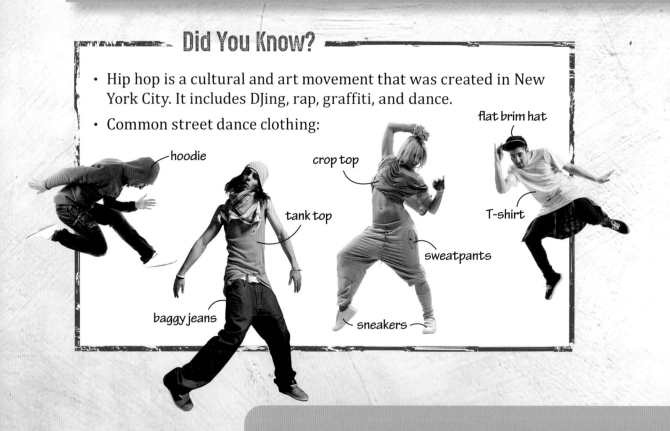

hoodie

flat brim hat

crop top

tank top

T-shirt

sweatpants

baggy jeans

sneakers

💬 What Do You Think?

- What are the positives and negatives of dancing?
- Do you think dance is an important part of a culture? Why?

Reading Comprehension

A. True or False

*Read the statements below and write **T** for true or **F** for false.*

_____ **1** Several popular dance styles were created in the 1960s.

_____ **2** B-boying/B-girling and popping started in the same club.

_____ **3** Popping involves contracting a desired muscle group.

_____ **4** The wrist twirl is a basic move in locking.

B. Multiple Choice

Circle the correct answer.

1 Which of the following is a step in the jack?

  a. Arch your lower back.

  b. Put your weight on the balls of your feet.

  c. Roll your neck.

  d. Place your feet hip-width apart.

2 What is true about b-boying/b-girling?

  a. It started in Chicago.

  b. It involves acrobatics moves.

  c. It involves lots of slow movements.

  d. The wrist twirl is a basic movement of this style.

3 Where was popping created?

  a. Los Angeles   b. New York

  c. Chicago   d. Miami

4 What is NOT true about Streetz: House of Hop?

  a. It has drop-in classes.

  b. It opens at 6:00 a.m.

  c. It opened in 1991.

  d. It offers classes on Saturdays.

Vocabulary Builder

A. Fill in the Blanks

Complete the sentences with the words and phrases below. Change the forms if necessary.

basic	heat	imagine	against
develop	bend	practice	take advantage of

1 I put the ladder _____ the wall.

2 We need to have more _____ for the show.

3 _____ you won the lottery. What would you do?

4 The recipe says to _____ the pan on high for two minutes.

5 I'll teach you some _____ salsa steps.

6 I'm going to _____ the sale and buy the game now.

7 The first smartphone was _____ in the 1990s.

8 Dennis couldn't _____ his arm for a few weeks after he broke it.

B. Words With Different Meanings

Match the word in bold with its definition.

1 _____ Please show us some **samples** of your work.

_____ The customers can **sample** three kinds of cake.

a. *n.* an example of something   **b.** *v.* to taste a small amount of something

2 _____ It's Jessica's **practice** to get up at six.

_____ How long is our **practice** going to last?

a. *n.* the activity of repeating something to get better at it
b. *n.* something people do often

3 _____ The teacher called the **roll**.

_____ The dancer **rolled** her arms in a snake-like way.

a. *v.* to move something like a wave in the ocean
b. *n.* an official list of names

Language Notes

Infinitives (to V.)

As a subject

- To learn math well <u>is</u> hard.
  ↘ singular be verb

  = It's hard to learn math well.

....

As an object

- Andy <u>wants</u> to go on a vacation this summer.
- <u>Try</u> to imagine you are dancing.
- My doctor <u>warned</u> me not to eat too much.
  ↘ not + to V.

Verbs followed by infinitives:

want	plan	decide
need	choose	ask
agree	tell	hope

- We **plan** <u>to finish</u> the report this month.
- Claire **asked** her child <u>to close</u> the door.

Your Turn

*Fill in the blanks with the given words. Change to **infinitive** forms.*

learn
finish
go
marry
exercise

❶ To stay healthy, Jody plans _____ every day.

❷ Edward promised _____ Bella and gave her a wedding ring.

❸ It is easy for me _____ English.

❹ My mother told me _____ my homework as soon as possible.

❺ We plan _____ on a trip abroad next month.

READING SKILL

Visualizing Text

Visualizing is the ability to create mental pictures based on what you read. It involves using your imagination and personal experiences.

Tips for visualizing text:

- Locate specific parts of speech to identify the objects and actions more clearly.
- Imagine the sight and even the sound, taste, smell, or feeling of something being described. Try to form a mental picture of the text.

Test Your Skill CD 27

Read the following introduction about Songkran. Try to visualize what the celebration is like and draw your mental picture below.

Songkran is the New Year celebration in Thailand. It starts on April 13th and goes to April 15th. During this celebration, there are big water fights all across the country. People use water guns, and they pour buckets of water on everyone.

Songkran and Chinese New Year have some traditions in common. People return home, clean their houses, and visit temples. However, they also pour water on their elders' hands to show respect. Today, they pour water on everyone else, too. It washes away all of the bad things from the past year.

PUT IT IN WRITING

TASK A

Read the flyer and answer the questions in full sentences.

1 What kind of dance lessons does Wagner's Dance Studio offer?

_____

2 When is the studio open on weekends?

_____

3 Would you like to take a lesson at this studio? What kind of dance would you like to learn?

_____

LET'S DANCE!

Lean techniques just like the pros!

We offer :
- ◆ Hip hop dance
- ◆ Ballet
- ◆ Ballroom dance
- ◆ Tap dance
- ◆ Cha cha

Wagner's Dance Studio is open from 10 a.m. to 9 p.m., Monday through Friday, and from 11 a.m. to 6 p.m. on weekends.

Call to book a session now! **1-800-123-456**

TASK B

Work in pairs. Look at the following painting closely and write a description about the painting. Then, share your description with the class.

89

UNIT 8

AVOIDING THE HARMS OF LIGHT

Learning Objectives

In this unit, you will . . .

- learn how to draw mind maps and connect ideas in a text.

> **Making connections:**
>
> *Think about how the ideas in a piece of writing are connected.*

- learn about the noun suffix *-ness*.
- learn about gerunds.
- create a mind map about using gadgets.
- write a paragraph based on your gadget mind map.

⏱ Get It Started

The following are some sources of light. Match the words to the correct pictures.
Then, write an A for artificial light and N for natural light.

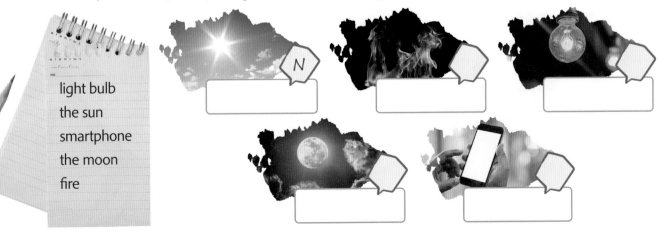

light bulb

the sun

smartphone

the moon

fire

Before Reading 🎧 28

Match the following words with their correct definitions.

❶ artificial · · a. a narrow line of light, heat or other energy

❷ harm · · b. the bottom part of a hat that sticks out

❸ link · · c. to reduce something to the least possible level

❹ minimize · · d. made by people

❺ brim · · e. a small tool that does something useful

❻ gadget · · f. damage

❼ ray · · g. to make a connection between two or more things

Scan the article. Then, write down the main points of the first five paragraphs.

Paragraph 1: _____

Paragraph 2: _____

Paragraph 3: _____

Paragraph 4: _____

Paragraph 5: _____

🎧 29

Light is great, isn't it? Rays from the sun keep us warm, put us in a good mood, and generally make life possible. Artificial light is also very important. Without it, everything would close at
5 sunset. However, there is a lot to suggest that too much light can do more harm than good.

You may already know about ultraviolet light. It is a high-energy form of light produced by the sun. This type of light is terrible for you. It can not
10 only give you a bad sunburn but also cause skin cancer and speed up aging over time.

To minimize risks, "slip, slop, slap, slide, and hide." That is, you should slip on dark or bright, loose-fitting clothing. Slop on some SPF 30+ sunscreen. Slap on a wide

15 brim hat. Slide on a pair of sunglasses. And, whenever possible, hide from the sun. Don't be fooled by clouds, either. UV rays have no problem reaching you even on cloudy days.

Once the sun sets, there's something else to look out

20 for—artificial light. Some examples are the light that comes from our smartphones, computers, and energy-efficient bulbs. Studies have shown that artificial light can influence our sleep cycles. For most of human history, we rose with the sun and went to bed soon after the sun went down.

25 Artificial lighting tricks us into thinking it is daytime. This light stops important chemicals from being made in our brain, like melatonin, which helps us sleep.

Loss of sleep has been linked to several health problems, such as cancer and heart disease. It

30 can also lead to mental illnesses. Getting a bad night's rest is especially bad for children. For example, it can make their memories worse.

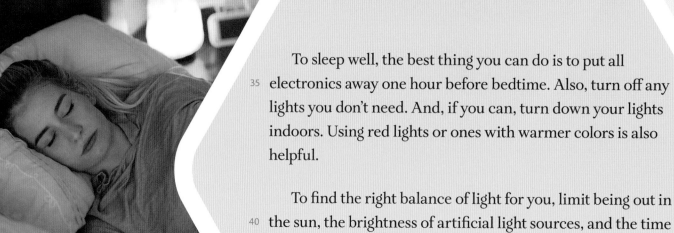

To sleep well, the best thing you can do is to put all
35 electronics away one hour before bedtime. Also, turn off any
lights you don't need. And, if you can, turn down your lights
indoors. Using red lights or ones with warmer colors is also
helpful.

To find the right balance of light for you, limit being out in
40 the sun, the brightness of artificial light sources, and the time
you spend with gadgets. Being sun-safe and keeping good
sleep habits will allow you to live your best life.

Did You Know?

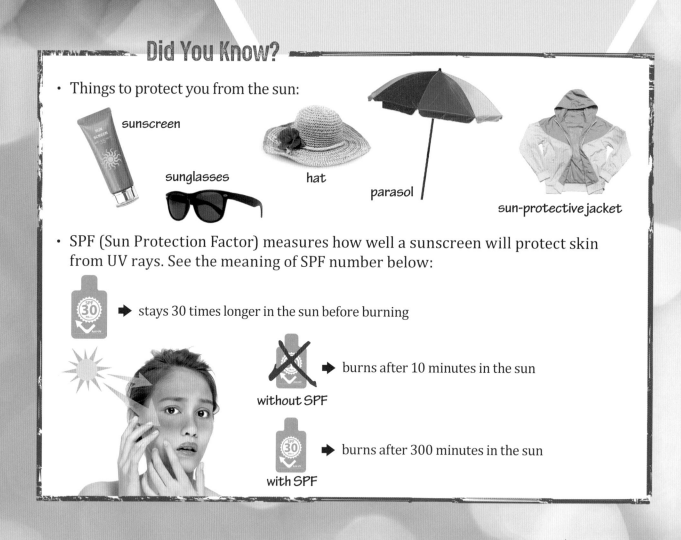

- Things to protect you from the sun:

sunscreen

sunglasses   hat

parasol

sun-protective jacket

- SPF (Sun Protection Factor) measures how well a sunscreen will protect skin
from UV rays. See the meaning of SPF number below:

➡ stays 30 times longer in the sun before burning

➡ burns after 10 minutes in the sun

without SPF

➡ burns after 300 minutes in the sun

with SPF

What Do You Think?

- What do you think life would be like if humans couldn't see any light?
- Do you think sunscreen can be harmful? Why or why not?

94

Reading Comprehension

A. Multiple Choice

Circle the correct answer.

❶ Why is ultraviolet light bad for our health?
    a. It can influence our sleep cycles.
    b. It can cause heart disease and cancer.
    c. It can cause skin problems like burns or cancer.
    d. It can make remembering things difficult.

❷ What does "slop" in "slip, slop, slap, slide, and hide" mean?
    a. Wear loose clothing
    b. Apply sunscreen
    c. Wear a wide-brim hat
    d. Stay in the shade

❸ Which is NOT a source of artificial light?
    a. The sun   b. Smartphones
    c. Computers   d. Energy-efficient bulbs

❹ According to the article, what should we do to help us sleep?
    a. Put all electronics away an hour before we sleep
    b. Turn on all the lights in the house
    c. Play soft music and take a hot bath
    d. Watch TV until we fall asleep

B. Short Answers

Read the following questions and write down your answers.

❶ Where does ultraviolet light come from?

_____

❷ How can artificial light affect our sleep cycles?

_____

❸ What should you do in order to find the right balance of light for you?

_____

Vocabulary Builder

A. Fill in the Blanks

Complete the sentences with the words and phrases below. Change the forms if necessary.

chemical	bright	terrible	without
limit	put away	habit	speed up

❶ Put your safety gloves on before you handle
_____.

❷ There's a _____ smell in the
living room.

❸ Keeping a diary is a good _____.

❹ This _____ red shirt will look wonderful on him.

❺ You will be very wet _____ your umbrella.

❻ You should always _____ your exposure to the sun.

❼ We need to _____ to complete the project.

❽ James opened the closet and _____ his coat there.

B. Suffix: -ness

The suffix -ness is usually used to make nouns from adjectives. Look at the examples in the left column. Then, complete the sentences with the correct form of words in the right column.

◎ · illness

· happiness

· loneliness

· kindness

❶ After Ray and Barbara were married, their friends wished them
_____. (happy)

❷ I like Robert because he's _____ and friendly (kind)

❸ Brad was _____, so he didn't go to school. (ill)

❹ To get rid of her _____, Patty decided to get a pet dog.
(lonely)

Language Notes

Gerunds (V-ing)

As a subject

• Playing cards with friends <u>is</u> fun.

       singular be verb ↰

• Traveling <u>makes</u> you happy.

      ↘ singular verb

As a complement

• Neil's favorite sport is swimming.

As an object of a verb

• Evan <u>enjoys</u> reading novels.

• Craig <u>practices</u> playing the piano every day.

As an object of a preposition

• I am interested <u>in</u> playing soccer.

Verbs followed by gerunds:

enjoy	keep	stop
finish	spend	mind
practice	quit	avoid

• They <u>finished</u> doing their homework.

• You should <u>stop</u> smoking.

Your Turn

Fill in the blanks with the given hints.

❶ I've asked Janet _____ to the party. (come)

❷ I enjoy _____ TV after school. (watch)

❸ My mom told me _____ my homework. (do)

❹ Would you mind _____ the door for me? (open)

READING SKILL

Making Connections

- Sometimes, a text may contain several ideas that must be connected to understand the
- "bigger picture." One of the best ways to collect and understand ideas is to use a mind
- map—a drawing that shows how pieces of information relate to one another. It usually
- starts with one word or idea at the center. Then, ideas that are related to it spread out
- from the center in degrees of importance.

Test Your Skill

Read the article Avoiding the Harms of Light again and complete the mind map below.

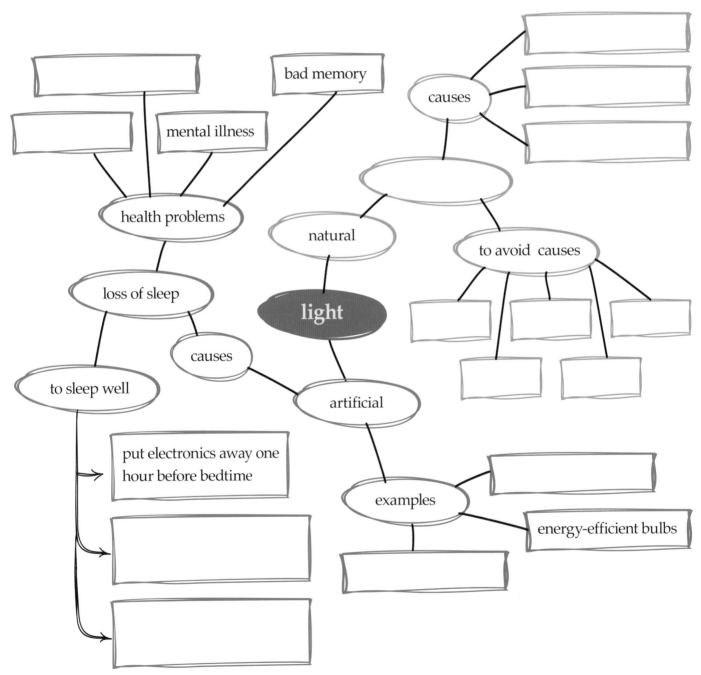

PUT IT IN WRITING

TASK A

Complete the following mind map about the positives and negatives of using gadgets.

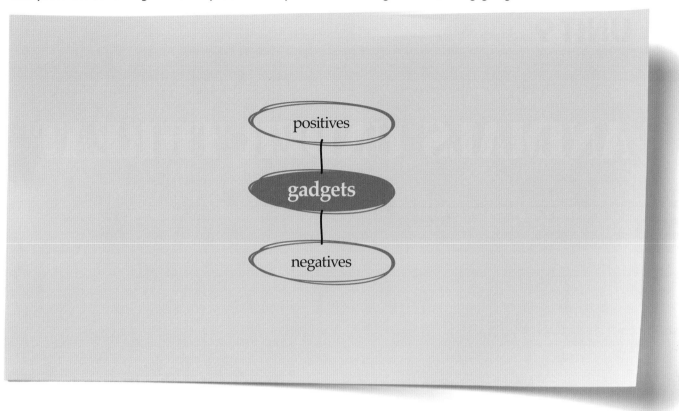

TASK B

Write a 100-word paragraph using the mind map you created in exercise A.

UNIT 9

ANIMALS UNDER THREAT

Learning Objectives

In this unit, you will . . .

- learn to recognize the cause and effect of an event or a condition.

> **Recognizing cause and effect:**
> *Read a text and identify the reason and result of a specific event or condition.*

- learn the names of some adult and baby animals.
- learn about comparative and superlative adjectives.
- write about three endangered animals' habitats and the reasons they are threatened.
- create a poster to help protect a threatened animal.

⏱ Get It Started

Complete the fast facts about the following endangered animals with the words and numbers below.

Asian elephant

Diet: grass, tree bank, roots, leaves, stems and _____

Size: Head to body—5.5 to 6.5 m; tail—1.2 to 1.5 m

Weight: _____ kg

Average Life Span in the Wild: _____ years

sea lion

Diet: fish, crustaceans, cephalopods and _____

Size: 2.4 m   Weight: _____ kg

Average Life Span in the Wild: 20 to _____ years

| 60 | 30 | penguins | 300 | bananas | 4,000 |

Before Reading 🎧 30

Match the following words and phrases with their correct definitions.

❶ countless ·   · a. animals and plants growing in natural conditions

❷ extinct ·   · b. one of several things that influence something

❸ prey ·   · c. an animal that is hunted for food by another animal

❹ factor ·   · d. not now existing

❺ fur ·   · e. because of

❻ due to ·   · f. very many

❼ wildlife ·   · g. the thick hair that covers the bodies of some animals

Scan the second paragraph. Identify three causes and their effects. Write down the clue words as well.

		Clue word:
❶ Cause:	Several kinds of human activities	
Effect:	Red panda's numbers have dropped.	because of
❷ Cause:		Clue word:
Effect:		
❸ Cause:		Clue word:
Effect:		

🎧 31

There are countless animals around the world. But did you know that many types of animals are becoming endangered due to different kinds of threats? In this article, we will cover three animals that are in danger of becoming extinct: the red panda, the Bengal tiger, and the blue whale.

Red Panda

Diet: Mainly bamboo

Size: Head to body—51 to 66 cm

   tail—25.4 to 51 cm

Weight: 4.5 to 9 kg

Average Life Span in the Wild: 8 years

5   The red panda isn't a large black-and-white panda. It's actually a small

animal that looks similar to a raccoon. These masked animals can be found in the mountains high up in trees or among the rocks. They mostly live in the Eastern Himalayas. Sadly, their numbers have dropped because of several kinds of human activities. Some people cut down forests, so red

10 pandas lose their homes. Others hunt red pandas for their fur or even to keep them as pets. Climate change is also a reason why they are at risk. Today, there are less than 10,000 red pandas left.

Bengal Tiger

Diet: Large animals such as deer and wild boars
Size: Head to body—150 to 180 cm
tail—60 to 90 cm
Weight: 110 to 225 kg
Average Life Span in the Wild: 8 to 10 years

Bengal tigers are the most common of all tigers. Most of them live in India and thus are also known as Indian tigers. Smaller numbers can

15 be found in Bangladesh, Nepal, Bhutan, China, and Myanmar. As the human population grows, the tigers are having more and more difficulty finding places for their homes. This then results in their low numbers. Another threat for tigers is hunting. Some people use tigers' body parts for traditional Chinese medicine. The loss of prey like deer and antelopes is

20 also a reason for the tigers' falling numbers. Currently, there are around 3,000 Bengal tigers left in the wild.

Blue Whale

Diet: Krill
Size: 25 to 32 m
Weight: Up to 181,000 kg
Average Life Span in the Wild:
80 to 90 years

krill

Blue whales are the largest of all animals on earth. One can weigh as much as 33 elephants. These giants of the ocean are the loudest of all animals. They are even louder than a jet engine. Most blue whales are

25 found in the Southern Ocean around Antarctica. Unfortunately, these grand animals are endangered with only 10,000 to 25,000 left. One of the factors is the loss of their main food source, krill—a tiny animal that looks like shrimp. Ship strikes and being caught by fishers have also caused the

numbers of blue whales to drop.

30   There is more wildlife that is in danger of becoming extinct. Forces like climate change and human activities such as clearing forests, farming, and hunting are all responsible for animal extinction. Though there is little that you as an individual can do to eliminate these major threats, you can

35 still make small changes to help. From reducing the damage you cause to the environment to helping conservation efforts, you can make a difference.

Did You Know?

- Red pandas use their long tails to stay balanced when climbing trees.
- It is likely that the name *panda* comes from the Nepali word for "bamboo eater."
- Bengal tigers are the national animal of India and Bangladesh.
- No two tigers have the same stripes.
- Blue whale calls reach 188 decibels, while jets reach 140 decibels.
- A blue whale eats about 3,600 kg of krill a day.
- The following shows a size comparison between a human, Bengal tiger, red panda, and blue whale.

1.8M

human   Bengal tiger   red panda   blue whale

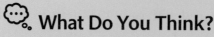

What Do You Think?
- Should people keep animals as pets? Why or why not?
- What do you plan to do to protect endangered animals?

Reading Comprehension

A. True or False

*Read the statements below and write **T** for true or **F** for false.*

_____ ❶ The red panda looks like a raccoon and is small in size.

_____ ❷ Serious weather changes are not a reason why red pandas are at risk.

_____ ❸ Most Bengal tigers live in Bangladesh.

_____ ❹ The body parts of a Bengal tiger are sometimes used for traditional Chinese medicine.

_____ ❺ The weight of a blue whale is similar to that of a jet engine.

B. Multiple Choice

Circle the correct answer.

❶ What is the main idea of this article?
   a. The life cycle of endangered animals
   b. The solution for animal extinction
   c. The reasons why some animals are endangered
   d. The diets of endangered animals

❷ How many red pandas are left?
   a. Around 2,500   b. Less than 10,000
   c. About 25,000   d. More than 40,000

❸ What is true about Bengal tigers?
   a. They eat large animals like deer and antelopes.
   b. They get along well with humans.
   c. They are also called Nepalese tigers.
   d. They normally live over 20 years.

❹ What do blue whales feed on?
   a. Fish   b. Seahorses
   c. Sea turtles   d. Krill

❺ The word "grand" in paragraph 4, line 26 is closest in meaning to "_____."
   a. Rare   b. Pretty
   c. Large   d. Important

Vocabulary Builder

A. Fill in the Blanks

Complete the sentences with the words and phrases below. Change the forms if necessary.

> main   weigh   avoid   climate   loss   among   similar   at risk

❶ The _____ in Africa is hot and dry.

❷ What's the difference? They look quite _____ to me.

❸ It takes time to get over the _____ of a pet.

❹ Fiona, a grown woman, only _____ 43 kilograms. She's too thin.

❺ James wanted to _____ an argument, so he kept silent.

❻ _____ all the students, Eddie often gets the best grades.

❼ Nancy doesn't understand the book's _____ idea.

❽ If you don't wear your seat belt, you'll put yourself _____.

B. Adult and Baby Animals

*Fill in the blanks with the correct baby animals: **cub**, **puppy**, **fawn**, **lamb**, **kitten**, or **duckling**.*

dog   cat   tiger

deer

duck   sheep

106

Language Notes

Comparative and Superlative Adjectives

$$A + be + \left\{ \begin{array}{l} \text{Adj.-er} \\ \text{more Adj.} \end{array} \right\} + than + B$$

- Cindy's hair is longer than mine.
  ↘ to compare two objects/states

- This book is more interesting than the other one.

$$A + be + the + \left\{ \begin{array}{l} \text{Adj.-est} \\ \text{most Adj.} \end{array} \right.$$

- Blue whales are the loudest of all animals.
  ↘ to compare more than two objects/states

- Being honest is the most important thing.

Your Turn

Fill in the blanks with comparatives or superlative adjectives.

❶ I'm _____ than my sister. (tall)

❷ Chemistry is the _____ subject for me. (difficult)

❸ The red flower is _____ than the white one. (beautiful)

❹ Rob is the _____ student in the class. (smart)

❺ Boiled food is _____ than fried food. (healthy)

READING SKILL

Recognizing Cause and Effect

A cause is a reason for an action or condition. An effect is the unavoidable result of a cause. To determine how a specific cause created a certain effect, we ask the question, "How did it happen?" or simply, "What happened?" We can also tell what a cause or an effect is by searching for words like *reason* or *factor*.

In some cases, linking words are used to create relationships between cause and effect. Here are some examples:

Cause	Effect
as, for, since, because, because of, due to, thanks to, on account of, owing to, resulting from	so, thus, hence, as a result, therefore, consequently, accordingly, lead to, result in, cause, bring about, give rise to

Test Your Skill

A. *Return to the article* **Animals Under Threat**. *Identify three more effects as well as the events that caused them.*

❶ Cause: _____

Effect: _____

❷ Cause: _____

Effect: _____

❸ Cause: _____

Effect: _____

B. *Create four sentences that show a cause and effect relationship using the linking words above.*

❶ _____

❷ _____

❸ _____

❹ _____

PUT IT IN WRITING

TASK A

List three more endangered animals, identify where they live, and write down the reasons why they are threatened.

	Animal	Where It Lives	Reason(s) for Endangerment
❶			
❷			
❸			

TASK B

Work in groups. Choose a threatened animal and create a poster to help save your chosen animal. Then, share your poster with the class.

Example

MINIMALISM: LESS IS MORE

 Learning Objectives

In this unit, you will . . .

- learn how to infer vocabulary while reading.

> **Inferring vocabulary:**
>
> *Read the text and infer the meaning of a word you're unfamiliar with.*

- learn collocations of *get*.
- learn about *that*-clauses.
- write about belief words with the suffix *-ism*.
- try minimalism for yourself and share your experience.

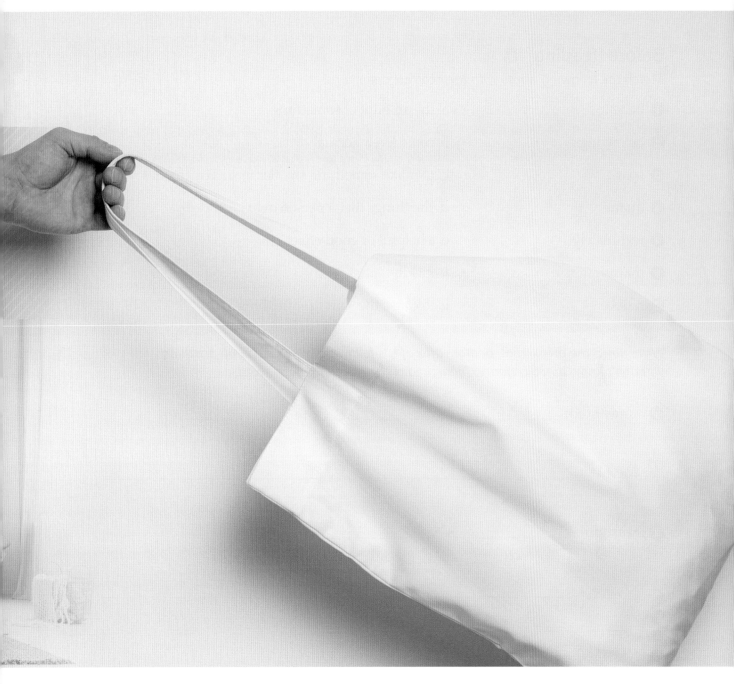

⏱ Get It Started

Look at the photos and answer the following questions:

- Which room would be better to live in? Explain your answer.

- Could you live in either room? Why or why not?

READING

Match the following words with their correct definitions.

❶ benefit   •   • a. the amount of something

❷ belongings   •   • b. considered normal

❸ spark   •   • c. to make something smaller in size or amount

❹ quantity   •   • d. the things that a person owns

❺ fortunately   •   • e. a helpful or good effect

❻ mainstream   •   • f. luckily

❼ reduce   •   • g. to cause the start of something

Write down the prefix, root, and/or suffix of the following words. Look up anything you don't know in a dictionary. Then, predict the meaning of the word.

❶ **unwanted:** _____ + _____ + _____
                   (prefix)   *(root)*   *(suffix)*

    Meaning: _____

- -

❷ **wasteful:** _____ + _____
               (root)   *(suffix)*

    Meaning: _____

- -

❸ **reuse:** _____ + _____
           (prefix)   *(root)*

    Meaning: _____

💿 33

    Many of us share a similar problem. We believe that buying more will make life easier. However, it often just makes life harder. We are overworked, own too much stuff, and have

no time to enjoy our lives. Fortunately, one solution has gone
5 mainstream—minimalism. This practice is all about learning to live
with fewer things, spend less, and value our belongings more.

The practice looks different for everyone. There's no right way
to be a minimalist. The important thing is to think long and hard
about what you need. That way you can remove unwanted items
10 and focus on only the things you care about, like family and friends.
Most people find that this makes them happier, healthier, and less
stressed.

Doing it is pretty simple. Maybe you have heard of Marie
Kondo—a famous author on minimalism. She says you should only
15 keep items that "spark joy in you." This is a good start. Look through
your things for anything you don't like or need. Then, you can either
sell or give those items away. Don't get rid of everything, as that can
be wasteful. Keeping practical and useful objects is just smart.

Next, you should cut down on shopping. Reuse items you
20 already own. Borrowing is also an option. The people around you
might have whatever you need, so ask them. However, if none of
this works, try to buy dependable objects that will last. This was a
common practice for our grandparents. They focused on quality
over quantity and expected the things they bought to outlive them.
25 Why shouldn't we?

The benefits of a minimalist life are clear. Living a minimalist life makes everything simpler and saves us time and money. The fewer things we have, the less there is to worry about. And,

30 all that extra time can be spent resting, having fun, or hanging out with loved ones. No wonder minimalists are so happy and relaxed.

Lastly, minimalism is good for the earth. Buying new things all the time does a lot of

35 damage. It makes global warming and pollution much worse. Practicing minimalism is one way to help to reduce waste. For our and the planet's well-being, minimalism shows us less is more.

Did You Know?

- The average American home contains about 300,000 items.
- An average American spends about $18,000 a year on unnecessary items.
- People don't wear at least 50% of what is in their wardrobes.
- On average, a British 10-year-old child owns 238 toys, but they play with only 12 each day.

What Do You Think?

- Do people generally own too much stuff? How much stuff is enough for you?
- Today, many of us spend too much time on social media. How can we apply minimalism to social media?

Reading Comprehension

A. True or False

*Read the statements below and write **T** for true or **F** for false.*

_____ ❶ The author believes it's important to think hard about what you need.

_____ ❷ People can become happier through minimalism.

_____ ❸ Minimalism encourages people throw everything away.

_____ ❹ People in the past valued quality over quantity.

_____ ❺ Minimalism is an expensive practice.

B. Short Answers

Read the following questions and write down your answers.

❶ What does minimalism encourage people to remove?

_____

❷ Who is Marie Kondo?

_____

❸ What does the author suggest doing to cut down on shopping?

_____

❹ How does minimalism help the planet?

_____

C. Identify Referents

Check what the following words in bold refer to.

❶ **it** (paragraph 1, line 2)
   ☐ work   ☐ buying more stuff   ☐ life

❷ **they** (paragraph 4, line 23)
   ☐ our grandparents   ☐ dependable objects   ☐ the people

❸ **it** (paragraph 6, line 35)
   ☐ global warming   ☐ the earth   ☐ buying new things all the time

Vocabulary Builder

A. Fill in the Blanks

Complete the sentences with the words and phrases below. Change the forms if necessary.

> extra focus value last pollution no wonder quality whatever

1 The children were allowed to do _____ they liked.

2 The teacher gave us _____ time to finish our homework.

3 I've been using the wrong password. _____ I can't log in.

4 Car exhaust is the main reason for the city's _____.

5 During my illness, I learned to _____ the ordinary things in life.

6 We need to _____ on our project.

7 The _____ of this bag is really good. It won't break easily.

8 My computer only _____ three months before it broke.

B. Collocation of *Get*

Complete the sentences with the correct collocations below. Change the forms if necessary.

> get rid of   get away from   get along   get together   get lost

1 _____ me! I'll call the police.

2 Lena is going to _____ her old scooter and buy a new one.

3 If you _____, check your map.

4 I don't _____ well with my brother.

5 Sandy and I will _____ this Sunday.

116

Language Notes

That-Clauses

> S. + V. + that + S. + V.

- Ms. Turner <u>said</u> <u>that she might run for the presidency</u>.
  ↳ as an object of a verb

- We <u>believe</u> <u>that buying more will make life easier</u>.

> S. + be + adjective + that + S. + V.

- Greg is <u>sad</u> <u>that his friend is going away</u>.
  ↳ as an adjective complement

- I am <u>suprised</u> <u>that Daniel has lost so much weight</u>.

> It + be + adjective + that + S. + V.

- <u>It</u>'s essential <u>that we finish this assignment today</u>.
  ↳ as a subject

Verbs before *that*-clauses:

find / believe / think / expect / hope / agree / say . . .

Adjectives before *that*-clauses:

angry / excited / happy / proud / sad / surprised . . .

Your Turn

Read the following sentences and add "that" to the correct spot.

❶ I hope they will say yes to my request.

❷ I was delighted Nick was chosen as our leader.

❸ Alexandra was happy her family was blessed with good health all year.

❹ Is it possible you send me your latest catalog?

❺ I agree we need more teachers for the school.

READING SKILL

Inferring Vocabulary

Identifying the root word and knowing the meaning of prefixes and suffixes can help you understand the meaning of new words. Here are some examples of common prefixes, suffixes, and their meanings:

Prefixes		Suffixes	
• *de-*	not, to remove or separate	• *-able*	capable, worthy of
• *dis-*	not, the opposite of	• *-ful*	full of
• *mis-*	wrong, bad	• *-less*	not having
• *pre-*	before	• *-ist*	someone who performs an action or believes in a particular set of beliefs
• *re-*	again, back to a former state		
• *un-*	not	• *-ism*	a social or religious belief, an act

Breaking down a compound word is another helpful tip. This type of word is formed by two or more words to create a new meaning. Some examples are *something*, *anyone*, and *moonlight*.

Test Your Skill

A. *Break down the following compound words into parts. Then, write the meaning.*

❶ **overwork:** = _____ + _____

Meaning: _____

❷ **outlive:** = _____ + _____

Meaning: _____

B. *Divide the following words by their prefix, root, and/or suffix. Then, write the meaning.*

❶ **disadvantage:** _____

Meaning: _____

❷ **dependable:** _____

Meaning: _____

PUT IT IN WRITING

TASK A

Work in groups. Research three belief words with the suffix -ism. Write down your findings.

Example

-ism: _minimalism_____   People who follow it: _minimalists_____

What it's about: _to live with fewer things, spend less, and value our belongings more_

❶ -ism: _____   People who follow it: _____

What it's about: _____

❷ -ism: _____   People who follow it: _____

What it's about: _____

❸ -ism: _____   People who follow it: _____

What it's about: _____

TASK B

Get rid of unwanted items in your room. Take a before and an after picture. Then, share how you feel after getting rid of those unnecessary items.

Before   After

_____

_____

_____

_____

_____

_____

YOU'RE JOKING, RIGHT?

⊕ Learning Objectives

In this unit, you will . . .

- learn to make inferences.

> **Making inferences:**
>
> *Read and draw conclusions based on implied information.*

- learn collocations of *out*.
- learn about the conjunction—*when*.
- write your own joke.
- make inferences based on a song or a poem.

⏱ Get It Started

- What makes you laugh? Is laughing good for you?
- What jokes do you know? Tell your partner.
- Look at the following words. What are the differences between them?

laugh giggle smile grin snicker

121

Before Reading 🔊 34

Match the following words with their correct definitions.

❶ scared   •   • a. nearly

❷ lick   •   • b. to cause someone to feel confused

❸ reward   •   • c. something given in exchange for good work

❹ puzzle   •   • d. afraid

❺ almost   •   • e. not real

❻ clerk   •   • f. someone whose job is to help people in a shop

❼ fake   •   • g. to move the tongue across the surface of something

Read the first joke "A Dog With Ideas" and questions below. Then, check (✓) the correct answers.

❶ **Why did the lion run away?**
- ☐ **a.** He thought he was in danger.
- ☐ **b.** He wanted to see some bones.
- ☐ **c.** He needed to lick his lips.
- ☐ **d.** He had to see the monkey later.

❷ **What did the dog want to make the lion believe in the end?**
- ☐ **a.** The dog wanted to talk to the lion.
- ☐ **b.** The dog planned to eat another monkey later.
- ☐ **c.** The dog asked the monkey to bring another lion to eat.
- ☐ **d.** The dog wanted to run away from the monkey.

🔊 35

A lion and a dog spotted each other in a forest. The dog was scared, but he saw some bones and got an idea. He licked his lips and said, "That was a delicious lion!" The lion got scared and ran away. A monkey saw everything. He wanted a reward, so he told the lion. They went to find
5 the dog together. When the dog saw them, he almost ran away. Then he got another idea "Where's that monkey?" he shouted. "I told him to bring me another lion an hour ago!"

A DOG WITH IDEAS

WHERE ARE WE?

Buuuuurrrrrrgerrrrrr Kiiiiiinnnnnng.

A man and his wife were driving across the U.S. on their vacation. One day, they arrived in a town called Kissimmee. The curious name puzzled them, and
10 they couldn't figure out how to pronounce it. In the town, they pulled into a place to get something to eat. In the restaurant, the man said to the clerk, "We can't figure out how to pronounce the name of this place. Could you tell me where we are? Say it very slowly so that I can understand." The clerk looked at him and said, "Buuuuurrrrrrgerrrrrr Kiiiiiinnnnnng."

FROZEN WINDOWS

15 It was a cold winter day. A man was at work when his wife called him. She was at home. "Something bad happened," she said. "Windows is frozen. What should I do?" "That's
20 easy," said the man. "Just get some very hot water and pour it on the windows." The wife said OK and hung up. Later, the man got a message from his wife. "I did what you said," it said, "but it didn't
25 work. Now the computer won't turn on at all!"

JUST LIKE MY BROTHER

Kelly was riding in a taxi. When the driver got to a stop sign, he didn't stop. He just went past it. Kelly looked worried, but the driver
30 said, "It's OK! I drive like my brother. He's a famous taxi driver." Then the driver ran through a red light. "Don't worry!" he said. "I drive like my brother." At a green light, the driver slowed down. This confused Kelly.
35 "Why are you slowing down? It's green!" she said. The driver answered, "I have to watch out. My brother may be coming the other way."

Did You Know?

- Our brains can tell the difference between real and fake laughter.

- Studies have shown that a person can laugh simply because someone else is laughing.

- An adult over 35 laughs about 15 times a day. A baby laughs about 400 times a day.

- Here is a funny riddle:
  What do you call a dog on the beach?

A: A hot dog

about 400 times

about 15 times

💭 What Do You Think?

■ Read the jokes again. Are they funny? What makes a joke funny?
■ Is humor different from culture to culture? Why?

Reading Comprehension

A. True or False

Read the statements below and write T for true or F for false.

_____ **1** In *Where Are We?*, the man and woman had no trouble saying the name of the restaurant.

_____ **2** In *Frozen Windows*, the computer stopped working.

_____ **3** In *Just Like My Brother*, Kelly was worried about how the taxi driver was driving.

_____ **4** In *Just Like My Brother*, the man's brother is also a taxi driver.

B. Multiple Choice

Circle the correct answer.

1 In *A Dog With Ideas*, what did the monkey tell the lion?

   a. He ate a delicious lion.

   b. He got a big reward.

   c. He went with the dog.

   d. All the things that he saw.

2 In *Where Are We*, what puzzled the man and his wife?

   a. The name of the town

   b. The people in the town

   c. The road in front of the restaurant

   d. The name of the restaurant

3 In *Frozen Windows*, what did the man's wife do in the end?

   a. She poured hot water on the computer.

   b. She turned off her computer.

   c. She asked someone to fix her computer.

   d. She threw the computer out.

4 In *Just Like My Brother*, how did the man's brother drive?

   a. He drove at the speed limit.

   b. He didn't stop for stop signs or red lights.

   c. He stopped at green lights.

   d. He drove very slowly.

Vocabulary Builder

A. Fill in the Blanks

Complete the sentences with the words and phrases below. Change the forms if necessary.

spot	curious	pronounce	hang up
riddle	confused	through	worried

❶ If you _____ any mistakes in the article, just mark them with a pencil.

❷ We walked _____ the restaurant but couldn't find our friends.

❸ How do you _____ this word?

❹ We need to hurry. I'm _____ that we'll miss our flight.

❺ My brother likes to tell jokes and _____.

❻ We were _____ by the signs on the road.

❼ The movie has a _____ ending.

❽ I'm going to _____ the phone now. Good-bye!

B. Collocations of *Out*

Complete the sentences with the correct collocations below. Change the forms if necessary.

figure out	watch out	give out	fill out

❶ Please _____ this sheet with a black pen.

❷ I can't _____ what the joke means.

❸ The clerk is _____ balloons to the kids.

❹ _____! The floor is very wet.

Language Notes

Conjunction—When

"When" is used to show that two actions are happening at the same time.

$$S. + \begin{Bmatrix} V. \\ be + V\text{-}ing \end{Bmatrix} + when + S. + \begin{Bmatrix} V. \\ be + V\text{-}ing \end{Bmatrix}$$

- Jack <u>ran away</u> when he <u>saw</u> me. = When Jack <u>saw</u> me, he <u>ran away</u>.
  ↘ a short action ↘ a short action

- The door bell <u>rang</u> when my mother <u>was cooking</u>.
  ↘ a short action   ↘ an ongoing action

  = When my mother <u>was cooking</u>, the door bell <u>rang</u>.

- I <u>was watching</u> TV when my father <u>came</u> home.
  ↘ an ongoing action   ↘ a short action

- My brother <u>was playing</u> video games when I <u>was studying</u>.
  ↘ an ongoing action   ↘ an ongoing action

Your Turn

*Combine the sentences using the conjunction **when**.*

❶ Bob stopped in front of the house. / He heard a strange sound.

Bob stopped _____

❷ Tiffany was sleeping. / The phone rang.

Tiffany _____

❸ I saw Mandy. / I was buying drinks at the convenience store.

When I was _____

❹ They were having a picnic. / It started to rain.

When it started _____

127

READING SKILL

Making Inferences

Making inferences means drawing conclusions based on implied information. To infer, we use information that is not directly written to figure out what the author implies.

Example:

> Max and his wife packed their winter clothes and everything they needed into their suitcases. They couldn't wait for this upcoming vacation. They had to get up early the next day and take the bus to the airport.

Information that is not directly written:
- Max is married.
- Max and his wife are going on a trip.
- The place they're going might be very cold.
- They are taking an airplane early on the next day.

Test Your Skill 🔊 36

Read the passage and choose the correct answer.

My favorite memory is my cousin's birthday party. It was a Sunday night in the fall. We gathered around a wooden table. I couldn't see much as the room was quite dark. I could smell the candles burning on top of the cake. I could almost taste the sweet sugar in the cake. I could feel the cool fall air on my skin. I could hear the gentle and sweet sound of the Happy Birthday song. It felt like joy and warmth inside the room.

❶ The author's cousin was born in (summer / fall).

❷ The light in the room was (on / off).

❸ The candles on top of the cake are (lighted / blown out).

❹ The party was held (indoors / outdoors).

PUT IT IN WRITING

TASK A

Create your own joke and try to include at least two points to make inferences from.

TASK B

Work in groups. Choose a song or a poem and make inferences. Then, share your work with your classmates.

Song / Poem:	Inferences:

UNIT 12

VR VS. AR: VISIONS OF THE FUTURE

⊕ Learning Objectives

In this unit, you will . . .

- learn how to compare and contrast while reading.

> **Comparing and contrasting:**
> *Read the text and identify similarities and differences between objects or events.*

- learn multiple usages of words found within the passage.
- learn about the passive voice.
- write about a technology that has changed the world.
- invent a new product.

(⏱) Get It Started

Look at the following photos and answer the questions:

- What is happening in these photos?

- Have you used any of this technology? Share your experience.

READING

Before Reading 🎧 37

Match the following words and phrases with their correct definitions.

❶ explore ·

 · a. to communicate with someone

❷ tell apart ·

 · b. to be not like something or someone else

❸ interact ·

 · c. to increase the amount, value, etc. of something

❹ differ ·

 · d. a person whose job is to sell houses and land for people

❺ augment ·

 · e. to search and discover

❻ virtual ·

 · f. made to appear to exist by the use of computer software

❼ realtor ·

 · g. to be able to see the difference between two very similar things or people

---

Scan the article. List three differences between VR and AR.

VR	AR
1	
2	
3	

🎧 38

Virtual reality (VR) and augmented reality (AR) are mentioned often these days. Experts say that these technologies are changing experiences of reality. Through them, people are exploring new worlds, changing their looks in photos, and training for real-life
5 situations. It is still hard to tell VR and AR apart, though.

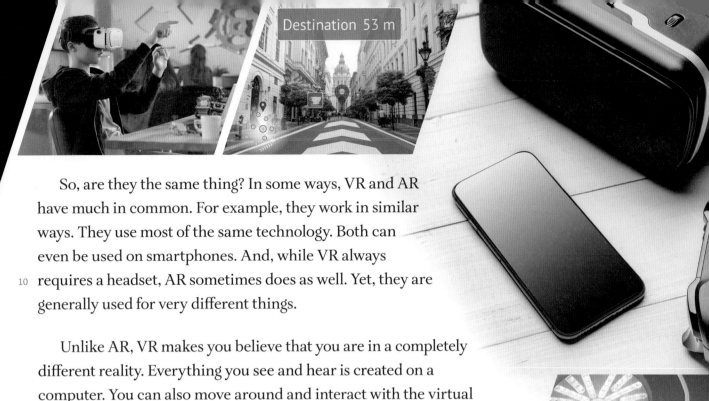

So, are they the same thing? In some ways, VR and AR have much in common. For example, they work in similar ways. They use most of the same technology. Both can even be used on smartphones. And, while VR always
10 requires a headset, AR sometimes does as well. Yet, they are generally used for very different things.

Unlike AR, VR makes you believe that you are in a completely different reality. Everything you see and hear is created on a computer. You can also move around and interact with the virtual
15 world with controllers. AR, on the other hand, doesn't take you anywhere. Instead, it brings digital objects into your world using a camera and screen. Pokémon GO, Google Translate's camera app, and Snapchat filters are good examples.

AR adds to your experience whereas VR changes it. This
20 makes both great for gaming. However, professionals have found different uses for VR and AR as well. Specifically, VR is a wonderful training tool. Pilots, doctors, and others use it to safely practice their jobs all the time. AR differs from VR in that it is easier to carry and cheaper. It is better for
25 working and sharing information with multiple people, too. Indeed, AR makes presentations and lessons much more interesting.

Many businesses also find that these technologies help sell items. By using VR, for example, shoppers
30 can now preview virtual kitchens at IKEA stores before buying anything. Realtors and travel agents are similarly using VR to give clients virtual tours of properties and locations. In contrast, AR has been

133

very useful to online stores. AR solves a huge problem
35 for these stores. It allows customers to try products
from home.

Each technology is powerful in its own way. VR
takes people to far and imaginative places, while AR
mixes the real and virtual worlds. Over the next few
40 years, they will only continue to advance. As they
advance, they will get smaller, less expensive, and
more capable. Most importantly, they will be able to
be applied in more areas. AR and VR have so much
potential. This is only the beginning for them.

Did You Know?

- Weird facts about Pokémon Go:
  - 👉 A man attached up to 67 smartphones to his bike to catch the creatures.
  - 👉 The creatures of this game have been found at some strange places; for example, in a war zone, on a plane, and even on a pet!
- Common VR devices:

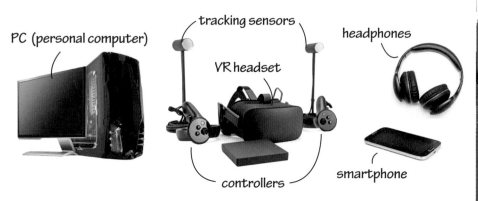

PC (personal computer) tracking sensors headphones VR headset controllers smartphone

💭 What Do You Think?

- For what else might AR and VR be useful? Give some examples and explain your answers.
- What other technologies have changed our experiences of the world? How have these technologies changed our experiences?

Reading Comprehension

A. Multiple Choice

Circle the correct answer.

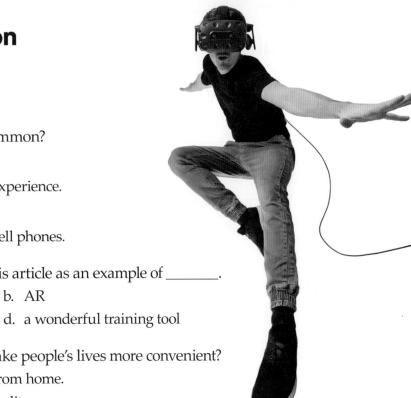

❶ What do VR and AR share in common?

    a. Both always require a headset.

    b. Both completely change your experience.

    c. Both use similar technology.

    d. Both must always be used on cell phones.

❷ Pokémon GO is mentioned in this article as an example of _____.

    a. VR   b. AR

    c. a completely different reality   d. a wonderful training tool

❸ What is one way that AR can make people's lives more convenient?

    a. Customers can try on clothes from home.

    b. People can take a break from reality.

    c. Doctors can help patients better.

    d. Pilots can practice their job.

❹ What is most likely true about AR and VR?

    a. The technologies will become more expensive.

    b. The technologies will be used in more situations.

    c. The technologies will become larger.

    d. The technologies will become less capable.

B. Short Answers

Read the following questions and write down your answers.

❶ How can people interact with the virtual world in VR?

_____

❷ What is the main difference between AR and VR?

_____

❸ What are the advantages of AR over VR?

_____

Vocabulary Builder

A. Fill in the Blanks

Complete the sentences with the words and phrases below. Change the forms if necessary.

> reality expert advance require capable add to product solve

1. The store is having a sale on all its _____.

2. This show will _____ the singer's growing reputation.

3. Riley's childhood dreams finally became a(n) _____.

4. Cell phone technology is _____ every day.

5. The students worked together to _____ the problem.

6. You are _____ to take a test before you can drive.

7. Jason is a(n) _____ in computers.

8. We need to get an assistant who's _____ and experienced.

B. Words With Different Meanings

Match the word in bold with its definition.

1. _____ The **object** of this game is to pick up as many balls as you can.

   _____ There was a strange **object** on the desk.

   a. *n.* a thing that you can see and touch and that is not alive

   b. *n.* the goal or purpose of a plan, activity, or action

2. _____ These regulations **apply** to all new employees.

   _____ Becky **applied** for the summer language program at the university.

   a. *v.* to have an effect on someone or something

   b. *v.* to ask formally for something

Language Notes

Passive Voice

We use the passive voice when we want to focus on the action in a sentence. It's not important to know who or what does the action.

S. + be + p.p. (+ by somebody)

- My wallet <u>was stolen</u>.
    ↳ We don't know who did the action.

- The windows <u>are cleaned</u> every day (by students).
    ↳ Students are not important here, and the word can be removed.

- The pyramid <u>was built</u> 5,000 years ago by ancient Egyptians.
    ↳ We want to emphasize **pyramids** more than **ancient Egyptians**.

Your Turn

Rewrite the following sentences using the passive voice.

❶ The typhoon caused great damage.

_____

❷ The neighbor invited us to the party.

_____

❸ I can finish the work by this Friday.

_____

❹ The police found the stolen car yesterday.

_____

137

READING SKILL

Comparing and Contrasting

We compare things to show how they are the same, and we contrast them when we wish to focus on their differences. Here are some key words to identify comparisons and contrasts from a text:

Comparing		Contrasting	
both	likewise	unlike	whereas
like	as	instead	while
same	as well (as)	yet	however
the same as	each	but	on the other hand
similar to	have in common	differ	although

Test Your Skill 🎧 39

*Read the passage below and circle the words that help you compare or contrast. Then, mark whether the following statements are true **T** or false **F**.*

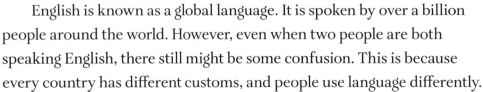

English is known as a global language. It is spoken by over a billion people around the world. However, even when two people are both speaking English, there still might be some confusion. This is because every country has different customs, and people use language differently.

Take Japan and the U.S.A. for example. People in these two countries often express opinions in different ways. In the U.S.A., people tend to be frank. If an American wants to reject someone's idea, that person will usually say "no." On the other hand, a Japanese person is less likely to say "no" as that might seem rude. Instead, he or she might say, "That would be difficult." When that person says this, it means "no." However, an American might misunderstand and say, "How can I solve the problem so you can say 'yes'?"

This example shows how English can be used in different cultures. If you have a similar problem, don't get upset. Instead, look at the other person's culture to understand what he or she is saying.

_____ ❶ People might misunderstand each other even though they both speak English.

_____ ❷ Americans think it's rude to say "no" directly.

_____ ❸ When a Japanese person means "no," he or she might say, "That would be difficult."

_____ ❹ Japanese people and Americans reject others' ideas in similar ways.

PUT IT IN WRITING

TASK A

Write about a technology that has changed the world. Complete the following information.

Technology:

_____

What the technology does:

_____

_____

Ways it has changed the world:

_____

_____

_____

TASK B

Work in pairs. Think of a product that doesn't exist. Give your invention a name, describe what it does, and draw what it looks like. Then, share your ideas with the class.

Name: _____

Description:

_____

_____

_____

(Draw your product)

Part A CD 40

Save the Hermit Crabs

In many cultures, crabs stand for change. People also believe they are good at protecting. That's because they have strong shells, and they change their shells as they grow bigger. Hermit crabs are famous __(1)__ this. They don't use their own shells, though. They use shells they find on the sand.

Many people keep hermit crabs as pets. They are quiet and cute. __(2)__, they are also very hard to care for. They need lots of water, lots of friends, and extra shells. Some people buy painted shells for their hermit crabs. This is not a good idea. The paint on the shells can slowly poison the crabs. A hermit crab in a cage usually lives for just a few months. In the wild, hermit crabs can live for over 30 years.

Hermit crabs are quite smart. If one finds a shell that is too big, it won't take it. It will wait until a __(3)__ crab passes by. If that crab is also too small, the crabs will form a line. When a crab that is the right size comes __(4)__, the crabs will trade shells one by one. Everyone gets a new home, and everyone is happy.

This only works if they can find shells. Humans often __(5)__ pretty shells at the beach. Because of this, there are fewer good shells for hermit crabs. Some are now making their homes in trash.

To help hermit crabs, we should leave shells alone. We shouldn't buy hermit crabs either. All pet hermit crabs come from the sea. They are happiest there.

A. *Choose the best answers to complete the text.*

_____ ❶ a. for   b. with
         c. as   d. to

_____ ❷ a. Also   b. Therefore
         c. Thus   d. However

_____ ❸ a. bigger   b. biggest
         c. more big   d. more bigger

_____ **④** a. along   b. across

                c. with   d. in

_____ **⑤** a. throw   b. give

                c. collect   d. change

B. *Read the passage again and answer the following questions.*

_____ **①** Why do people think crabs are good at protecting?

     a. Because they're quiet and cute.

     b. Because they're good at fighting.

     c. Because they have strong shells.

     d. Because they are big.

_____ **②** The underlined word "their" in the third line of paragraph 2 refers to "_____."

     a. the painted shells'   b. the people's

     c. the hermit crabs'   d. the friends of hermit crabs'

_____ **③** Which of the following is NOT true about hermit crabs?

     a. They need lots of water.

     b. Painted shells are not good for them.

     c. They can live for over 30 years in the wild.

     d. They usually make their own shells.

_____ **④** What would a hermit crab do if it finds a shell that is too big?

     a. Take the big shell   b. Wait for a bigger crab to take it

     c. Walk away   d. Hide the shell

_____ **⑤** What happens when there are fewer good shells for hermit crabs?

     a. They are kept as pets.

     b. They take painted shells instead.

     c. Some of them make their homes in trash.

     d. They trade shells one by one.

_____ **⑥** What can we do to save hermit crabs?

     a. Stop buying them   b. Pick and sell shells at the beach

     c. Change homes for them   d. Put them in a cage

Keeping Safe from Smog

Air pollution, or smog, is __(1)__ kind of pollution. It's not only bad for the earth but also bad for our health. About seven million people die each year because of it.

Smog is dangerous because it's hard to avoid. On bad days, it's everywhere. If you go outside, you will breathe it in. If you breathe in too much, you will get sick. Today, people are working to reduce smog. Hopefully, there will be less of it in the future. Until then, though, you need __(2)__ yourself.

Sometimes, smog is hard to see. So, you __(3)__ check your area's air quality each day. There are apps that help you check if the air is bad. Many people wear masks on bad days. However, masks vary in quality. Unless you have a highly effective mask, bad air can get through. A better idea is to stay inside. __(4)__ your windows and use an air filter. If you have to go out, limit your time. __(5)__ plants in and around your home can also help as plants clean the air.

Though air pollution is hard to avoid, you can do a few things to keep safe. It doesn't have to stop your life so long as you are safe.

A. *Choose the best answers to complete the text.*

_____ ❶ a. worst   b. the worst
         c. worse   d. the worse

_____ ❷ a. protect   b. protects
         c. to protect   d. protecting

_____ ❸ a. should   b. mustn't
         c. shall   d. will

_____ ❹ a. Closing   b. To close

                c. Closes   d. Close

_____ ❺ a. Grown   b. Grows

                c. Growing   d. Grow

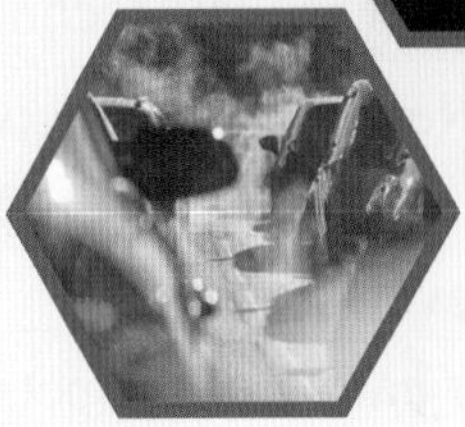

B. *Read the passage again and write **T** for true or **F** for false.*

_____ ❶ Air pollution is hard to get away from.

_____ ❷ Millions of people are killed by smog each year.

_____ ❸ You can see smog easily.

_____ ❹ Using an air conditioner is a good way to avoid smog.

_____ ❺ Plants can help us by cleaning the air.

C. *Read the following questions and write down your answers.*

❶ Why is smog dangerous?

_____

❷ What will happen if you breathe in too much smog?

_____

❸ How can you know if the air is bad?

_____

❹ Why isn't wearing a mask a good way to protect yourself from smog?

_____

❺ How can you protect yourself from air pollution if you need to go out?

_____

Cared for by Robots

People are living longer and longer these days. That's good news. It's great to have a long life. However, it's hard __(1)__ old. Many people get sick and need care. When there are many elderly people in society, finding care is difficult. Today, technology is helping us __(2)__ this problem.

New robots can give elderly people all kinds of care. Some of them lift and move people from bed to bed. Others help people around their homes. There are even some __(3)__ can just be good friends. The simplest robots used for elder care are like pets. __(4)__ you touch them, they will move or make animal sounds. They bring real joy to elderly people, and no one has to feed them.

Some elder care robots use AI. The robots tell people when to take pills, exercise, and see the doctor. They make video calls to family members. Also, if the robot's owner is in trouble, the robot will call someone for help. Other care robots do physical jobs. They pick things up, help people walk, and lead groups in dances. Japanese hospitals use these now. The people there like them a lot.

Many of these robots don't just help elderly people do things. They also help them feel useful and independent. Some companies make their robots look weak. They look __(5)__ they need care. That way, people will care for the robots while the robots care for them.

A. Choose the best answers to complete the text.

_____ ❶ a. to get   b. is getting
            c. gets   d. get

_____ ❷ a. finish   b. fix
            c. use   d. make

_____ ❸ a. also   b. either
            c. that   d. though

_____ ❹ a. When   b. How
            c. That   d. What

_____ ❺ a. for   b. at

                        c. up   d. like

B. _Read the passage again and answer the following questions._

_____ ❶ What problem is mentioned in the first paragraph?

     a. Many elderly people live alone.

     b. People get old faster.

     c. It's hard to find care for elderly people.

     d. Everyone gets sick more easily.

_____ ❷ Which of the following is NOT mentioned about robots in the passage?

     a. They can help elderly people around their homes.

     b. They can feed elderly people's pets.

     c. They can lift and move elderly people from bed to bed.

     d. They can make elderly people happy.

_____ ❸ What can care robots do using AI?

     a. Make video calls   b. Remind people to take pills

     c. Tell people to see a doctor   d. All of the above

_____ ❹ What will a care robot do when its owner is in trouble?

     a. Take them to the hospital   b. Give them pills

     c. Call someone for help   d. Move them to a bed

_____ ❺ What is true about care robots?

     a. They are used in Japanese hospitals.

     b. People have to feed them.

     c. They can teach people how to walk.

     d. They can only do physical jobs.

_____ ❻ Why are some companies making their robots look weak?

     a. To make elderly people feel weak   b. To help elderly people carry them easily

     c. To make elderly people trust them   d. To help elderly people feel useful

FAKE?

TRUE?

MAYBE?

Stop Fake News

You are checking Facebook. Among the funny cat videos, vacation photos, and silly cartoons, you see a news article. It says __(1)__ scientists just discovered a new kind of fruit. Juice from the fruit can cure cancer in just two days. That sounds amazing! You think you should share the article with your friends. But, you should think again. That article is almost certainly a fake news story.

These days, it's easy __(2)__ these kinds of articles all over Facebook and other websites. Some of them are jokes. Others want you to assume that they're true. Spreading these articles isn't a good idea, either. Fake news writers get money every time someone clicks on their articles. That's good for them. However, it's bad for us. Fake news can <u>bring about</u> serious problems.

The Internet is a great place to learn new facts. However, you shouldn't assume that everything on the Internet is true. Websites can be __(3)__ by anyone. People can post real news onto these websites, or they can post false stories. It's up to you to __(4)__ the difference.

Before you share a news story, ask yourself a few questions about it. Does it seem too crazy to be true? Does it make you feel a strong emotion? If it does, it may be fake news. Is any other website reporting the story? Are any of those websites well-known? If not, you should probably ignore the story for now. Fake news isn't going to go away. If we're smart, though, we can stop fake stories __(5)__ they do any damage.

A. *Choose the best answers to complete the text.*

_____ ❶ a. which   b. when
         c. that   d. what

_____ **②** a. to find   b. finds

                c. find   d. found

_____ **③** a. create   b. created

                c. creating   d. to create

_____ **④** a. ask   b. throw

                c. know   d. allow

_____ **⑤** a. because   b. unless

                c. before   d. until

B. _Read the passage again and answer the following questions._

_____ **❶** The underlined phrase "bring about" in the fifth line of paragraph 2 is closest in meaning to "_____."

     a. add   b. discover

     c. become   d. cause

_____ **❷** What can be inferred from the statement "you shouldn't assume that everything on the Internet is true"?

     a. You shouldn't read every article on the Internet.

     b. You shouldn't use the Internet too often.

     c. Some stories on the Internet are false.

     d. It is suggested to learn new facts through the Internet.

_____ **❸** In which case should you ignore a news story?

     a. When the story seems too crazy to be true

     b. When the story is reported on many other websites

     c. When the story doesn't make you feel a strong emotion

     d. When the website that posts the story is well known

Note

Note

LINGUAPORTA

リンガポルタのご案内

> **リンガポルタ連動テキストをご購入の学生さんは、「リンガポルタ」を無料でご利用いただけます！**

　本テキストで学習していただく内容に準拠した問題を、オンライン学習システム「リンガポルタ」で学習していただくことができます。PCだけでなく、スマートフォンやタブレットでも学習できます。単語や文法、リスニング力などをよりしっかり身に付けていただくため、ぜひ積極的に活用してください。

　リンガポルタの利用にはアカウントとアクセスコードの登録が必要です。登録方法については下記ページにアクセスしてください。

https://www.seibido.co.jp/linguaporta/register.html

本テキスト「Active Reading Strategies Book 1」のアクセスコードは下記です。

7286-2048-1231-0365-0003-007a-3SU4-SWD3

・リンガポルタの学習機能（画像はサンプルです。また、すべてのテキストに以下の4つの機能が用意されているわけではありません）

● 多肢選択

問題 2
英文を完成させるのに最も適切な語句を選びましょう。

Computers are useful, _____ they may also cause various health problems.
○ but　　○ so　　○ because　　○ and

　　　　解答する

● 空所補充（音声を使っての聞き取り問題も可能）

問題 3
音声を聞き、空所に適切な語を入れましょう。

▶ ⏸

Experts say some workers _____ in their jobs, many have found new one _____ after reshuffling throughout the past few years. But _____ is staying put of their own volition. Some workers still _____ , but with a slowdown in uncertain economic forecast.

　　　　解答する

● 単語並びかえ（マウスや手で単語を移動）

問題 3
日本語の意味となるように、与えられた語を下線の上に並べ替え、文を完成しましょう。

私の両親は、私が一人で休暇に行くことを許可しました。
My parents [　　　　　　] vacation alone.

| me | on | allowed | go | to |

　　　　解答する

● マッチング（マウスや手で単語を移動）

問題 3
Match the following English with its Japanese definition.

complain	（労力・時間・金など）を節約する
celebrate	（こと）を制限・限定する
restrict	満足させる
save	〜を祝う
satisfy	不平（不満・文句）を言う

　　　　解答する

151

TEXT PRODUCTION STAFF

edited by	編集
Takashi Kudo	工藤 隆志

cover design by	表紙デザイン
Ryoichi Kawarada	川原田 良一

DTP by	DTP
Ryoichi Kawarada	川原田 良一

CD PRODUCTION STAFF

recorded by	吹き込み者
Howard Colefield (AmE)	ハワード・コールフィルド（アメリカ英語）

Active Reading Strategies Book 1

2024年1月20日　初版発行
2024年2月15日　第2刷発行

著　　者　　角山 照彦
　　　　　　LiveABC editors

発 行 者　　佐野 英一郎

発 行 所　　株式会社 成 美 堂
　　　　　　〒101-0052　東京都千代田区神田小川町3-22
　　　　　　TEL 03-3291-2261　FAX 03-3293-5490
　　　　　　https://www.seibido.co.jp

印刷・製本　（株）加藤文明社

ISBN 978-4-7919-7286-9　　　　　　　　　　　　Printed in Japan